To Flo and Jane

Counselling skills
FOR DOCTORS

Sam Smith and
Kingsley Norton

Open University P
Buckingham · Phila

Open University Press
Celtic Court
22 Ballmoor
Buckingham
MK 18 1XW

email: enquiries@openup.co.uk
world wide web: http://www.openup.co.uk

and
325 Chestnut Street
Philadelphia, PA 19106, USA

First Published 1999

A catalogue record of this book is available from the British Library

ISBN   0 335 20014 1 (pb)   0 335 20015 X (hb)

Library of Congress Cataloging-in-Publication Data
Smith. Sam. 1951–
    Counselling skills for doctors/Sam Smith and Kingsley Norton.
        p.   cm.
    ISBN 0-335-20015-X. – ISBN 0-335-20014-1 (pbk.)
    1. Mental health counseling. I. Norton, Kingsley. II. Title.
  RC466.S64   1999
    610.69′6–dc21   98-34015
                                                                      CIP

Typeset by Graphicraft Limited, Hong Kong
Printed in Great Britain by The Cromwell Press, Trowbridge

Contents

Acknowledgements

Between us, in the twenty or so years since medical qualification and in our separate clinical settings, we have engaged in thousands of clinical transactions with those who, willingly or unwillingly, have been our patients. Some patients we will have seen only once, and for a few minutes at that. Others we have spent hours and hours with, sometimes over months and even years. Many of these patients, but also friends, colleagues, trainees and students, too numerous to name, have contributed to the rich experience of our professional lives as doctors. We wish first to pay our thanks to them, since it is from this experience that the thoughts and ideas contained in this book have been distilled.

We owe a special debt of gratitude to Flo Smith and Jane Fisher-Norton for their support and encouragement, for their critical reading of various drafts and for making so generously the very real sacrifices of space and time which allowed us to complete this book. We are likewise ever grateful to Richard and Teresa Adair, Liz Agnew, Richard Brook, Chris Dowrick, Alex Esterhuyzen, David Fainman, Fiona Ford, Frances Mair and Branwen Martin, who have all made particular contributions in one way and another, and with whom we share our professional lives.

We first encountered Professor Arthur Crisp at St George's Hospital Medical School when being introduced to the complexities of psychiatric medicine. We would like especially to thank him for agreeing to write the foreword and being interested enough to take the time and trouble to do so. Thanks are due to other medical educators, in particular Dr Gordon Wright of Clare College, Cambridge, who had a formative part to play in our professional development.

Debbie Jones, Kathy Stewart, Julia Wilding and Jenny Woodward also deserve our gratitude for their generous and good-natured help with recalcitrant word-processors, photocopying and fax machines and for typing numerous drafts of fledgling chapters.

Michael Jacobs approached us to write this book and throughout has evinced nothing but confidence in our ability to produce the goods. We thank him for his careful reading of the text and for his useful and encouraging comments. Thanks too are due to Jacinta Evans and Joan Malherbe at the Open University Press. Any deficiencies that remain are ours alone.

Foreword

Our personal and public selves are variably relevant to all of us as we negotiate our way through life. Self-awareness of their mainsprings should be part of adult mental equipment. But such a universal property becomes especially powerful, with the potential for seriously good or bad effects on others, when wielded within prescribed and important public roles – none more so than that of the medical practitioner; for instance the general practitioner whose relationship with his patients is enduring.

The public licenses the 'doctor' to invade the body and readily and remarkably permits such intimate access. The doctor's primary responsibility is expert knowledge of and familiarity with that body; the public presumes this to be the case and, moreover, that the doctor has the patient's interests at heart. It is this trust, usually called upon at times of crisis, that renders the medical consultation unique in its potential impact.

Invasion of the body might narrowly be construed in such terms as palpating its surfaces and cavities, incising and puncturing it, introducing chemicals into it, transfixing it with wave formations. But the mind, that infinitely complex and elusive process, but with its principal apparatus firmly rooted in the brain, is also part of the body.

The public brings its distress in many forms to the doctor. For instance the panic that accompanies a mortal threat or mental disorder itself. And such presentations may be more than usually oblique or not apparent at all. The doctor's licence requires that he or she is as knowledgeable of and familiar with examination of the mental state as with the respiratory and cardiovascular systems. Moreover, it is through verbal and non-verbal communication with the patient that the doctor engages in the consultation.

Assessing the significance of historical information, sensing information withheld, listening to and formulating the problem, examining the mental state itself, informing and advising the patient, primarily involves the doctor's and the patient's minds. Seemingly simple procedures like the giving of advice or support require that element of self-awareness and the capacity thereafter to moderate personal attitudes and feelings. Counselling and communication skills, in which even limited processes like the giving of advice are embedded, require that such subjectivity is harnessed to the task of helping the patient to change, whether this be simply to enable greater mental resilience or, more ambitiously, to develop new coping skills.

Doctors asking themselves whether the acquisition of such counselling skills needs to be or should be part of their generic competence can reflect on the chemistry of memory, the neurotransmitting properties underlying organization of the mind and the influence of learning and unlearning on such processes. Change wrought by them can sometimes be more enduring and sometimes more effective than the temporary introduction of psychotropic medication.

The communication skills required for medical practice have an unnatural element to them. Communicating in the interests of others, outside the intimate family, is perhaps less common than communicating for self-promotion or commercial or political success. As the authors point out, the word 'doctor' derives from the Latin word for teacher. Doctors and teachers share the task of enabling others to acquire knowledge and skills. The authors, acting as both teachers and medical practitioners, have written an economic and simple account that achieves this goal. They steer clear of all jargon whilst paying homage to the clinical wisdom of relationship-based psychotherapy. They base their case on the distinction between public and personal roles for both the doctor and the patient, and the need for the doctor to harness the related forces and their interaction to good psychological purpose for the patient, within the boundaries of reality.

They illustrate their thesis with good everyday 'case' material. 'Danny', 'Mrs Bradley' and the others play their parts well.

Their consistently simple style and logical course encourages the kind of reflection that can best promote insight. This is a text that can provide a good basis for teachers, vocational trainers and students of medicine at all educational levels. It is clearly not an esoteric text targeting only specialists in mental disorder; nor is it only relevant to general medical practitioners. It is especially important for the super-specialist tempted to focus exclusively on part of some other organ or bodily system. It is a text that should find its counterpart and meanwhile can subserve that purpose within other groups such as the law, the police, the teaching profession, and it is also a text suitable for that seminal phase of life, secondary education. That both authors were students at St George's Hospital Medical School is, at the least, a tribute to that school's selection procedures.

Professor A.H. Crisp
Emeritus Professor of Psychological Medicine,
St George's Hospital Medical School, London, and
Chairman of the Education Committee of
the GMC 1982–88

Introduction

In the unconscious, there is no such concept as 'health'. There is, however, a concept of 'death', and, in our constant attempts to keep this anxiety repressed, we use various unconscious defensive mechanisms including the creation of social systems, to serve the defensive function. Indeed, our health service might more accurately be called a 'keep-death-at-bay' service.

(Anton Obholzer 1994: 171)

The best kind of patient . . . is one who from great suffering and danger of life or sanity responds quickly to a treatment that interests his doctor and thereafter remains completely well; but those who recover only slowly or incompletely are less satisfying.

(Tom Main 1957: 129)

This is a book about the **intrinsic counselling skills** doctors need to bring to their consultations with patients. It is not a book about counselling of the sort undertaken by professional counsellors, even though the role of counsellor is sometimes taken on by doctors in the course of their work. Rather it is about those skills which, together with clinical, communication and teaching skills, doctors deploy in order to guide the consultation towards a successful outcome. A successful consultation, or clinical transaction, depends on something more than the doctor arriving at a correct clinical diagnosis, albeit couched in physical, psychological and social terms. Usually it depends also on both doctor and patient being reasonably personally satisfied with the contribution each has made towards the process of arriving at that diagnosis. If they are, then this helps form the basis of a therapeutic alliance which is fundamental to the subsequent management of the problem in which both have a continuing part to play.

The professional role of a doctor is socially constructed and hence imbued with relatively stable and predictable attitudes and expectations. Similarly, there are attitudes and expectations concerning what it is to be a patient and the appropriate performance of that role within the clinical transaction. Much of the process of the clinical transaction is guided by this professional framework in which the roles of doctor and patient are, at least in theory, complementary and supportive of one another. If it happens that doctors and patients do not share expectations of the clinical transaction and how each role should be fulfilled, these matters may well need to be negotiated afresh.

Beyond professionalism, however, the more personal aspects of doctors matter to patients and, needless to say, the personal attributes of patients are equally important to doctors. The personal relationship between patient and doctor has a significant, sometimes profound impact on the success or otherwise of the clinical transactions in which they engage. The clinical transaction, therefore, is pursued on both **public** (including professional aspects) and **personal levels**. At the public level, doctors and patients perform their roles as doctor and patient, with the aim of defining, solving and managing the problem presented by the patient. Within limits imposed by these public roles, they also interact at a personal level and, as with any relationship, doctors and patients are capable of gelling or clashing. The personal level interaction, therefore, has the potential either to support and sustain the work at the public level or to undermine and sabotage it. Personal and public levels of the clinical transaction constantly interact.

Monitoring and assessing the progress of the public level of the transaction is, at least in most of its aspects, a routine task. If puzzling aspects remain they can usually be addressed by retaking a history or repeating an examination or investigation. Sometimes, however, more stubborn and less obvious difficulties arise within the public domain. They are often attributable to misunderstandings concerning the terms in which doctors and patients couch their accounts of illness and disease or to differences in expectations about its management and where responsibility for this lies.

At the personal level matters are a lot more complex for a number of reasons. There are many aspects of personality which affect the ways that people habitually relate to others. People are often unaware of attributes of their personality and how they affect their relationships with others. An individual patient's overt friendliness and apparent willingness to cooperate, for example, may hide a deeper mistrust or lack of confidence that any help asked for will be forthcoming. Very often it is the interaction of personalities, rather than an attribute of just one person's personality, which is important. The effect of such 'hidden' factors at the personal level may become manifest only within the public domain, as when patients fail to attend for follow-up or do not comply with treatment.

Any problems arising from the interaction at the personal level may well be masked by the constraints imposed by the public level interaction. Doctors are supposed to be affable, trustworthy and respectable, and patients, respectful, truthful and compliant. Equally doctors are supposed not to be seductive, belligerent or mistrustful. To the extent that doctors and patients perform their public roles well, any underlying contradictory or conflicting attitudes or feelings within the personal domain may well be correspondingly harder to discern.

Doctors may not have been specifically trained to be alert to evidence that aspects of their personal relationships with their patients are affecting the clinical transaction. Indeed, they may not be fully aware of the significance of the personal level of clinical transaction for the achievement of the transaction's goals. Even if sensitive to these matters, they may not have training in how to deal with them within the clinical transaction. Patients, for their part, however sensitive they may be to the quality of the relationships with their doctors, are generally unlikely to take them to task if they find them unsatisfactory. The imbalance of power which usually pertains within the clinical transaction makes this difficult.

In spite of these potential problems, probably the majority of clinical transactions proceed relatively straightforwardly to an appropriate outcome, acceptable to both patient and doctor. That they do so is testimony to the usually robust reciprocal social roles of 'doctor' and 'patient' (which help to ensure active collaboration during the clinical transaction) and to the doctor's successful deployment of consulting skills. In these circumstances clinical transactions are characterized by an appropriate balance between the demands of the public level activity and the quality of the interaction between patient and doctor at the personal level. The latter should be sufficiently concordant and empathic to support and sustain the sometimes arduous and distressing work of the clinical transaction. We call the appropriate balance of public and personal aspects of the clinical transaction its **functional public–personal equilibrium**.

If the public–personal equilibrium of the clinical transaction is not preserved there are two dangers. First, personal level factors may become so prominent as to threaten to distract attention from (or even overwhelm) the public level work of the clinical transaction. This is obvious when tempers are lost, for example, or when doctors and patients become sexually involved. However, disturbances in the equilibrium of the clinical transaction can be much more subtle than this. Second, a deficient connection with the personal level may render serious, even life-threatening aspects of the public level work devoid of their proper emotional significance. If this happens, the result may well be that the motivation and commitment necessary for the appropriate management of the problem is seriously undermined.

Maintaining a functional equilibrium requires doctors to be aware of those factors likely to upset it and vigilant for any evidence of their effects. This means that at the same time as engaging in the necessary clinical work of the transaction, doctors need also to monitor the process of the clinical transaction on both public and personal levels. Any out-of-the-ordinary or inappropriate feelings or events, at either level, whether felt within themselves or observed, should alert doctors to the possibility that the appropriate public–personal equilibrium is threatened. Having identified and located the problem, they are then in a position to intervene if need be. The process of monitoring and regulating the clinical transaction in this way depends on the deployment of **intrinsic counselling skills**.

Intrinsic counselling skills come more easily to some doctors than others. Deploying them demands knowledge about how personality and consulting style is capable of influencing clinical transactions with particular patients or when facing certain types of problem. Self-awareness, insight and sensitivity with regard to the feelings and circumstances of others are essential. It is sometimes held that these attributes are intuitive, dependent on aspects of personality which cannot be taught, and that, in any case, they are irrelevant to the work of diagnosing and treating disease. The evidence suggests otherwise.

In this book we aim to make the concept of intrinsic counselling skills clear and to show how they are a routine and essential part of consulting. Used effectively they can make the difference between the success or failure of a clinical transaction. They are put into action from the moment doctor and patient first meet and are relevant at all stages of the transaction from history-taking to the diagnosis and management of the patient's problem. They have a wider relevance too both in terms of how doctors work effectively together as teams and also as agents within the broader systems of health care.

In Chapter 1 we review consulting skills. There is ample evidence that good communication is important for the success of clinical transactions. We introduce the concept of intrinsic counselling skills and briefly describe the kinds of intervention that doctors use to facilitate and deepen communication and to enhance educative aspects of the clinical transaction. These include those ways of listening, attending and responding which come under the usual rubric of general counselling skills.

We outline a model of the clinical transaction in Chapter 2, introducing and defining the important distinction between **straightforward** and **complicated clinical transactions**. Intrinsic counselling skills are employed to preserve straightforward and avoid complicated transactions. When difficulties arise during a consultation, defining and locating the problem can be difficult. The task is facilitated by using the **transaction window**, a diagrammatic representation of the clinical transaction which divides it into public and personal levels. We give examples of how it can help doctors dissect and analyse complicated transactions and so decide how best to intervene to put matters right.

In Chapters 3 and 4 we explore the different phases of the diagnostic process, namely history-taking, examination and investigation.These phases are marked by changes in the balance of power within the clinical transaction. Each phase is likely to require different modalities of enquiry, language, touch and investigative technology, which have both general and individual implications for patients and doctors. Whatever its phase, the clinical transaction proceeds as always on two levels which the doctor must try to harmonize. Intrinsic counselling skills are, therefore, as important during physical examination as they are at any other stage. In these chapters we begin to draw attention to the fact that patients and doctors belong to groups or systems outside the clinical transaction itself which, nonetheless, can exert a profound influence on it.

Chapter 5 reviews those aspects of the clinical transaction which, following the diagnostic phase, help doctor and patient to manage the problem successfully. We explore the important concept of the therapeutic alliance between doctor and patient and discuss impediments to cooperative management, together with ways of avoiding them. Clinical examples illustrate how intrinsic counselling skills can be used effectively. The importance of paying attention to the endings of clinical transactions, for example when patients are discharged from hospital, is emphasized.

Health promotion is an increasingly important activity for doctors. In Chapter 6 we draw attention to the fact that, when it comes to matters of health rather than disease and its management, the doctor's knowledge and expertise are more open to question. Lifestyles, for which patients are deemed to be responsible, are nowadays regarded as important determinants of health. Educating and advising patients about what they should do to optimize health is one thing but changing an unhealthy lifestyle is another. We contend that empowering patients to make difficult changes demands particular sensitivity both to the balance of personal and public aspects of the clinical transaction and to the influence of outside systems, such as peer groups, families and the media. Intrinsic counselling skills are therefore particularly important if health-promoting activities, as part of the clinical transaction, are going to be effective.

The implication of patient and doctor also belonging to separate systems which nonetheless impinge on the clinical transaction is explored in some detail in Chapter 7. Here we look at what is involved in being part of a team. Much of a doctor's working life is spent as a member of one sort of team or another. We examine how the different levels in the hierarchy of health care interact, ultimately to influence the clinical transaction itself. Intrinsic counselling skills deployed by the doctor within the clinical transaction depend on an ability to monitor public and personal levels. This ability is shown to be equally valuable when applied to the systems, such as the multidisciplinary clinical team, which impinge on clinical transactions. This is particularly true in circumstances where the team is engaged in treating patients with psychiatric or personality disorders, as some of the clinical examples amply illustrate.

The notion of intrinsic counselling skills, together with the theoretical approach to the clinical transaction, is nowhere more important than in the matter of training doctors, from medical students onwards. Chapter 8 outlines implications for training at all stages. We point out that it is not only the clinical transaction between patient and doctor that is marked by being pursued on public and personal levels and which can be construed as either straightforward or complicated. It is also true of the relationships between teacher and pupil or consultant and junior doctor, in which both formal and personal aspects coexist. We believe that these relationships, including relationships within peer groups, are an hitherto underexploited educational resource. They can be used to explore and illustrate the complex interaction of public and personal levels, between individuals and in groups. By encouraging and facilitating self-awareness, the intrinsic counselling skills required to harmonize the demands of the different levels of interaction can be formally taught and developed. We argue that this goes hand in hand with education about the sociological and psychological factors which influence attitudes and behaviour.

In the concluding chapter we examine the difficulties faced by training institutions and individual doctors in coming fully to grips with the implications of a two-level model of the clinical transaction. Alongside clinical skills, the ability to communicate effectively and sensitively and to build empathic, functional relationships with patients, patients' families and with professional colleagues is nowadays regarded as essential. Even so, the teaching of the relevant interpersonal skills still struggles to find adequate time and space in the crowded medical curriculum. We explore the nature of this difficulty suggesting that it is, in part, due to unconscious psychological defences against anxieties evoked when dealing with issues at the personal level.

Chapter 1

Consulting skills

All the power of tongue and pen, and all the wisdom of textbook and lecture can never teach a doctor the knowledge of when to probe and when to leave alone, when to chide and when to reassure, when to speak and when to keep silent. They are private mysteries with a different solution for every one of the million permutations of personality involved between a doctor and his patient.

(Richard Asher 1972: 113)

Introduction

These words of Richard Asher were given in reply to an opening address by Michael Balint at a meeting of the Medical Section of the British Psychological Society in 1955. Since that time his 'private mysteries' have come under close examination and, while perhaps falling short of providing solutions, this has at least offered useful insight into those aspects of a doctor–patient relationship which Asher maintained could not be taught. Nowadays talk of communication and counselling skills is commonplace and indeed such skills are taught to increasing numbers of students – the very stuff of 'when to speak and when to keep silent'. Books on such topics abound and are testimony to Richard Asher's own belief that 'the way we deal with our patients, and especially how we talk to them, is about the most important part of our trade' (Asher 1972: 112).

There is convincing evidence that good communication is of practical importance in improving compliance with and the efficacy of treatment, as well as contributing to the satisfaction of patients. Of poor communication the converse has been shown to be the case (Horder and Moore 1990). It also seems to be true, contrary to Asher's assertion and in justification of all relevant training courses, that communication skills can indeed be taught (Innui *et al.* 1976; Bird *et al.* 1993).

Nonetheless, some private mysteries do remain. The interaction between individual patient and doctor is, in important respects, a unique permutation of different personalities. At a personal level the interaction between patient and doctor has far-reaching implications for the pursuit of the clinical task, whatever that may be (Norton and Smith 1994). Individual reactions to asking for, giving or receiving help, in part determined by past experience, profoundly affect the way patients present their illnesses to doctors, their expectations of what is to happen and, in turn, the way doctors respond. We argue that it is in this area that certain counselling skills, and not merely communication skills, are necessary for effective consulting.

The consultation

Every culture has had its medical men and women seeking to alleviate the 'suffering of fellow humans from disease in a unique, intensely private, one-to-one relationship' (Ko Ko 1993: 54). Traditionally this has involved the submission of the patient to the authority, knowledge and skills of the doctor. Nowadays there is some redress in the balance of power within the consultation, at least as far as recognizing the need for patients to play an active role in understanding and dealing with their illness. Sociologists of medicine have been critical of the doctor's assumption of power and the monopolization of the definitions of health, disease and treatment. They argue persuasively that lay knowledge and understanding not only may be rational, but also should be taken into account by doctors if the medical task is to succeed (Armstrong 1986; Tuckett *et al.* 1986).

Not only is the one-to-one relationship within medicine changing but so too are the institutions of health care. The evolution of medicine as a collective enterprise, together with scientific developments that make medicine more effective but also more costly, has meant that the role of medicine in society has taken centre stage in economic and political terms. In the UK since the late 1980s there have been dramatic efforts to change the face of health care, to limit costs, empower the patient and offset professional medical power. This has reflected a shift in emphasis away from the sanctity of the one-to-one relationship towards public health, disease prevention and health promotion (see Chapter 6). As long ago as 1913, however, Sir William Osler proclaimed that 'the actual care of the sick, once our sole duty, is now supplemented by such a host of other activities, such as scientific, administrative, that an ever-increasing number of our members have nothing to do with patients as such' (quoted in Ko Ko 1993: 59). The expanded role of the doctor makes the acquisition of good communication skills no less an imperative part of training. We would argue that certain counselling skills are equally necessary. They are also pertinent to managerial relationships, general practice, hospital settings and the sphere of public health.

Consulting skills

In the words of James Spence, 'the essential unit of medical practice is the occasion on which in the intimacy of the consulting room or sick room a person who is ill, seeks the advice of a doctor whom he trusts. This is a consultation and all else in the practice of medicine derives from it' (quoted in Wright and MacAdam 1979: 3). Beyond bringing to the consultation the necessary attitudes of enquiry, respect and the desire to be of help, the doctor's task is to ascertain the reason for the patient's attendance, agree the problem and its probable causes and negotiate a plan for managing it.

To this end, within an appropriate setting, a history is discovered, an appropriate physical examination performed, further investigation carried out, a diagnosis or list of possible diagnoses offered, and a problem and its treatment mutually defined. Where patients are referred by another doctor it is no less important that the patient's account is attended to. Should more than advice, information or support be required suitable treatment can then be decided on, in the hope or expectation that this will be effective and within the scope of both patient and doctor to accomplish. Additional enquiry into other relevant aspects of the patient's life and health may be made and discussed if appropriate and time allows (Stott and Davis 1979).

Besides basic professional attitudes and a stock of scientific and clinical knowledge, a range of skills is employed by the doctor in pursuing this task. There are many ways of characterizing these skills. The Royal Australian College of General Practice, for example, derives five consulting skills: knowledge (the ability to recall facts); interpretative skill; problem-solving skill; appropriate attitudes, interpersonal and communication skills; and perceptual and manual skills (Fabb and Marshall 1983). Others divide the consultation into interview and exposition and describe the key skills as: questioning; listening; responding; and explaining (Preston-Whyte 1987). Concerning the skills required for the delivery of family medicine, the following skills are considered crucial: problem-solving; preventive; therapeutic; and resource management (McWhinney 1981). Most lists inevitably cover much the same ground, albeit with a different emphasis and theoretical orientation.

Communication and teaching skills are seen primarily to be concerned with the rational exchange of relevant information, i.e. at a purely cognitive level. The specific aims are to delineate the problem and establish a sufficient degree of mutual understanding to allow appropriate clinical management to follow. In addition, and by contrast, certain counselling skills address feelings and attitudes attendant on the exchange of information, including some which may not be immediately open to the conscious awareness of the patient. Factors operating at this affective, interpersonal level of the consultation can sometimes muddy communication and impede progress towards a successful outcome.

Such counselling skills are an essential adjunct to effective communication and teaching in so far as they help clarify, remove or minimize any affective impediments to communication and learning. However, they are also useful in monitoring the overall quality of the interpersonal relationship between patient and doctor within the consultation. Using these 'intrinsic' counselling skills helps doctors to maintain this relationship as one of sufficient mutual trust and respect to sustain the often painful or distressing work of the consultation.

Clinical skills

Clinical skills refer to a knowledge of what is normal and what abnormal, and those skills of history-taking, performing physical examinations and deploying investigative techniques necessary to distinguish between the two and to account for the difference. In addition, knowledge and skill are required in choosing a suitable plan to manage the problem, tailored to its particular manifestation in an individual patient. Acquiring evidence-based clinical skills to a certain level is the major part of a doctor's training. Without such a grounding we would not be modern doctors at all.

Communication skills

'Communication with his patients and colleagues is central to all that a doctor does. Yet it is such an everyday activity that it is often taken for granted; and doctors rarely pause to consider its pitfalls – or the trail of misunderstanding it is prone to leave behind' (Wright and MacAdam 1979: 61). Good communication is acknowledged to be as essential for effective consulting as are good clinical skills (General Medical Council (GMC) 1993). Poor communication can undermine the best clinical work and make the difference between success and failure.

Successful consulting depends on doctor and patient achieving a sound, mutual understanding of the presented problem and its management. Accomplishing this entails recognition of those factors which facilitate and those which obstruct such understanding. Knowledge of these factors and the central importance of good communication, following the pioneering work of Michael Balint, has been a focus of teaching and research in general practice particularly (Pendleton and Hasler 1983; Myerscough 1992). The lessons to be learned, however, are of equal value to surgeon, physician and psychiatrist alike.

Communication skills are those which are utilized to ensure that what is meant is what is understood (Curzon 1990). In a two-way process, attention is focused on the clarity of the message, which needs to be audible, unambiguous, free of jargon, concise and couched within compatible systems of belief so that lay and medical understanding can be integrated. Any doubts about meaning should be clarified and checked periodically. Elements of importance should be stressed and recapitulated to facilitate their recall at some future time. Non-lexical aspects of speech such as tone, intensity, rhythm and speed, and non-verbal signals (including body-language and use of space) should be concordant with and not contradict the message (Curzon 1990).

Style

No matter how rational and diligent the attempt to follow rules of good communication, something personal to each communicator also inserts itself among the spoken words. It is this personal element, perhaps, that Richard Asher referred to as being unteachable and its practical importance is captured in the familiar aphorism, 'it's not what you say, but the way that you say it'. Style silently betrays underlying attitudes and attributes such as confidence or the lack of it. It is remarkably constant for an individual doctor across many consultations with different patients (Byrne and Long 1976). There is no doubt that style affects communication (Pendleton and Hasler 1983) nor that it is closely dependent on deeply ingrained aspects of personality (Norton and Smith 1994).

It must be remembered, however, that different people respond to a particular doctor's style in different ways. Some patients may feel comfortable with a no-nonsense manner which others find off-puttingly brusque. Similarly, patients have different styles of presenting their complaints and it is as much the compatibility of styles as a particular style itself that is important for communication (S. Smith 1997). One of the potential strengths of group general practice is that patients, based on their experience, can often choose to consult the doctor with whom they get on best, at least outside emergency appointments. Where no such choice is possible, as in most hospital settings, there is greater onus on the doctor to safeguard good communication.

Style, in its conscious and unconscious manifestations, integrates the personal and public faces of the doctor. Work on training courses, with professional actors taking the part of patients or doctors, however, provides convincing evidence that style can be pure performance (McAvoy and McAvoy 1981). Acting might therefore be added to the list of consulting skills and doctors encouraged to perform in a style designed to optimize effective communication. But clinical experience teaches that under the everyday pressures of consulting, any actor's mask is bound to slip. Indeed, evidence suggests that most doctors do not even attempt to change styles to suit their patients and, for example, remain consistently more or less doctor-centred or patient-centred (Byrne and Long 1976). Even so, accepting style as given, and within a given style, evidence also demonstrates that the skills of communication can be taught and learned (Bird *et al.* 1993).

Teaching skills

The word 'doctor' derives from the Latin *docere*, meaning to teach. A significant aspect of a doctor's relationship with a patient is educational in its aim. In many respects this is a two-way process as doctors must also be prepared to learn from their patients. Important in performing the professional role, however, is the education of patients about the clinically relevant aspects of health and illness.

Good communication is essential for effective teaching but the aims of teaching go beyond simply getting the message across. Teaching can be defined as 'a system of activities intended to induce learning, comprising the deliberate and methodical creation and control of those conditions in which learning does occur' (Curzon 1990: 18) and learning as 'the apparent modification of a person's behaviour through his activities and experiences, so that his knowledge, skills and attitudes, including modes of adjustment, towards his environment are changed, more or less permanently' (1990: 10).

Learning, to some degree, is implicit in every patient's understanding of and adaptation to their illness. It includes learning to be compliant with treatment and modifying health-seeking behaviour (Stott and Davis 1979). Learning to take on the fullest responsibility for managing an illness demands from patients a high degree of accomplishment, especially where chronic conditions are concerned. The doctor as teacher has the task of facilitating this process. Most doctors learn about how to teach (and sometimes not even then in any formal way) only when they take on the task of training other doctors. Teaching skills, however, are just as relevant in the consulting room.

A doctor's teaching involves not only transmitting information but also taking care that the patient can retain and recall it. In addition, the patient must have some motivation to learn. In this respect the objectives of learning must be held in common by both doctors and patients. Learning objectives can be divided into three domains: the cognitive, concerned mostly with knowledge and information; the affective, relating to attitudes, emotions and values; and the psychomotor, involving muscular and motor skills. Of clinical relevance is the observation that the most frequently encountered blocks to learning are to be found in the affective domain, i.e. to do with feelings and emotions (Curzon 1990). The subject matter of the consultation is always personal, often distressing and contact can be of extreme intimacy – psychologically and physically (see Chapter 4). It is not surprising, therefore, that the affective domain is of particular importance in the doctor–patient relationship. It is in relation to this domain that a doctor's intrinsic and general counselling skills play such a crucial part of the consultation.

Counselling skills

Nowadays, counselling is a commonplace part of general practice and hospital work, and indeed the world at large. Upwards of 38 per cent of general practices offer on-site counselling services in a variety of forms (Curtis-Jenkins 1996). Counsellors are a diverse group owing allegiance to several different theoretical schools. Among the most important of these are: psychodynamic – deriving from Freudian theory and stressing the importance of a dynamic unconscious; behavioural – of whom the most important luminaries were perhaps John Watson and B.F. Skinner, who sought to account for human behaviour in terms of stimulus-response theory and reinforcement; cognitive – advanced by psychologists such as Dewey, Bruner and Vygotsky, emphasizing processes of thought and perception; and humanistic – Carl Rogers's person-centred approach, seeking to escape the more deterministic psychologies that had until then held sway. For a fuller account of these and other schools of thought see Curzon (1990) and Burnard (1989) or refer to the abundant literature on the subject (e.g. McLeod 1993).

Most doctors are not trained counsellors, although many doctors will assume a counselling role on occasion. Patients, however, may be aware of a qualitative difference between a 'counselling style' of consulting compared to a routine clinical enquiry or the provision of information or prescriptive instructions (Farrall 1993). Counselling skills have been identified and prioritized by doctors as a learning need (Phongsavan *et al.* 1995) and their use has been advocated as a means of improving the quality and effectiveness of consulting, particularly in cases of psychological distress or mental illness (Corney 1993).

We have already characterized counselling skills as those needed to address the personal, often subliminal, aspects of the interaction with the patient, in so far as these are relevant to clinical work. As such they demand self-awareness as well as sensitivity towards and empathy for the patient. They entail a non-reductive, holistic and imaginatively enquiring attitude reflected in a patient-centred consulting style. In broad terms they can be divided into two kinds: listening and attending; and verbal counselling interventions (Burnard 1989). A similar account describes basic techniques in terms of listening and observing, and various kinds of more active response (Jacobs 1988).

Listening and attending

Studies have repeatedly shown that doctors, on the whole, are not good listeners. The average listening time before interrupting the patient has been quoted at about 18 seconds. Yet when allowed to talk without interruption, 98 per cent of patients take less than two minutes to describe their complaint (Wilkinson 1989). In terms of counselling skills, listening not only means keeping quiet, thereby allowing the patient to talk without interruption, but also means keeping an ear open to recurrent themes and to words or phrases when tone or mood seem to change or fluency falters. All may signify unspoken anxieties or interpersonal difficulties and betray a narrative in which the present problem is but an incident. The fullest picture of the patient's problem can be achieved only by paying close attention of this kind. Time taken to listen is well spent. Not only does it improve diagnosis, but also patients who feel they have been listened to are more likely to cooperate with treatment (Corney 1993).

While listening, the doctor's focus of attention should include non-verbal communications from the patient, which may support or apparently contradict what is spoken. Close attention is necessary as well for remembering what has been communicated. If listening for any length of time much material must be held in memory if it is to guide responses later on. Doctors must also direct their attention inwards, monitoring their own responses and reactions to what the patient is communicating. Finally, they must remain attentive to the adverse influence of any external intrusions, pressure of time, other matters in hand or perhaps their own personal problems.

Responding

Counselling responses of different types fall broadly into two categories (Heron 1975; Burnard 1989). They can be either authoritative ('I tell you') or facilitative ('Can you tell me?'). Within the category of authoritative interventions are:

- prescriptive interventions – where a particular line of action is recommended
- informative interventions – where information or instruction is given
- confronting interventions – where some contradictory feature of a patient's account or aspect of behaviour is challenged.

Such interventions are common especially in doctor-centred consultations where the doctor's agenda is given priority (Byrne and Long 1976).

Facilitative interventions are also of three varieties:

- cathartic interventions – encouraging and allowing space for the release of emotion

- catalytic interventions – interventions designed to keep the patient's account going or to achieve greater depth, such as questions, particularly open ones, or reflections
- supportive interventions – affirmative of the patient's account, actions or emotions.

Facilitative interventions are more common in patient-centred consultations but it is important to recognize that it is likely to be a judicious balance of both sorts of intervention which is necessary for a successful consultation.

Another categorization describes responses covering much the same ground (Jacobs 1988). These include reflecting and exploratory responses – similar to catalytic interventions. They move the patient's account along and seek to draw out something extra. They can also buy time for the doctor to consider further responses. In addition, there can be information-seeking and informing responses and linking responses. These latter seek to make connections between elements in the patient's account and, if accurate, can bring to awareness and make sense of feelings or conflicts which are part of the patient's predicament.

An old proverb states that 'He who will not be counselled, cannot be helped'. In the context of the proverb, to be counselled means to receive advice, and giving advice is undoubtedly part of a doctor's job. Counselling, however, is a more complex process than it might appear. For advice to be effective, more is entailed than simply telling a patient what to do. We have already touched on the important issues of non-verbal communication, style, problems of affect and motivation, as well as other attributes of individual personality which can influence the course of a clinical transaction. Many of these aspects interact, not only affecting doctor and patient at a personal level, but also affecting the progress of the more public clinical tasks. If the transaction is to be successful, therefore, doctors need to monitor events at both levels as the clinical transaction proceeds (Norton and Smith 1994).

The monitoring of the interaction within and between public and personal levels of the clinical transaction, and how this interaction affects the progress of the transaction overall, requires what we refer to as 'intrinsic' counselling. This surveillance of the clinical transaction is essential if doctors are to do what they can to ensure that the transaction achieves appropriate goals. Like the other consulting skills discussed above, intrinsic counselling skills can be taught and learned so that they become an integral part of consulting. We shall develop our understanding of intrinsic counselling throughout the book and particularly in the next chapter where it is placed in the context of a two-level model of the clinical transaction.

Conclusions

The consultation lies at the heart of medical practice. The process of successful consulting demands that doctors engage in a range of activities which require certain skills. Many of these consulting skills are essentially clinical. If the consultation is to be effective in securing desired clinical goals, however, the patient must be involved with the doctor in a collaborative endeavour. Doctors need additional and complementary skills, therefore, which are directed towards fostering and securing such a 'therapeutic alliance' with the patient. These must include the ability to communicate effectively and to educate patients about aspects of their illness and its management, skills which in turn depend on and are supported by a range of counselling skills.

Doctors and patients are people with distinct personalities and styles of consulting. How they interact with each other at a personal level can influence the process and outcome of the consultation. This interaction is further influenced by the nature of the problems that patients present. Individual doctors and patients may well have idiosyncratic emotional responses to particular problems. In order to sustain the capacity of doctor and patient to work effectively and collaboratively on the clinical problem, their interaction at this personal level must be sufficiently harmonious. Endeavouring to ensure that it is and remains so, therefore, is an important task for doctors during the consultation.

Success at this latter task is facilitated by the use of what we call intrinsic counselling skills. These skills are not purely intuitive and can be taught and learned. The notion of intrinsic counselling skills can be more clearly grasped in the context of the model of the consultaion, or clinical transaction, which will be developed in the next chapter.

This chapter started with some words of words of Richard Asher's. His further thoughts make an appropriate conclusion.

> To give a patient the impression you could spare him an hour, and yet make him satisfied within five minutes, is an invaluable gift, and of much more use than spending half an hour with him, during every minute of which he is made to feel he is encroaching on your time. I do not know if this special kind of unhurried placidity can be acquired purposely, but it is a most enviable faculty to possess.
>
> (Asher 1972: 117)

Chapter 2

Intrinsic counselling skills and the clinical transaction

> Apart from an undeniably better understanding of the patient the 'deeper' diagnosis has another function. This is the reduction of the number of cases in which the doctor has to take a blind decision based only on a physical diagnosis. Such blind decisions, hardly influenced by the patient's emotional situation and by a proper control of the doctor–patient relationship, allow free play for the doctor's personal bias, unconscious sentiments, firm convictions and prejudices.
>
> (Michael Balint 1964: 68)

Introduction

Particularly since the work of Balint there has been a common perception that a consultation proceeds essentially on two distinguishable but interconnected levels – one more superficial, the other deeper. In this chapter we introduce and develop a two-level model of the clinical transaction between doctor and patient which aids our understanding of the place and function of intrinsic counselling skills. These skills are deployed to ensure that the different depths within the clinical encounter are each borne in mind. Such skills are needed because the interaction between the different levels adds complexity to the clinical transaction. The model we propose helps the doctor dissect this complex, interactive, two-person system, revealing opportunities for other strategic counselling interventions should these be needed.

At the more superficial and overt level of the consultation a problem is presented, a diagnosis made and treatment or advice offered. Doctor and patient perform their respective roles in the clinical transaction as doctor and patient. But there is a deeper level to the consultation (Balint 1964). Doctors and patients are also people, with personal lives, feelings and preoccupations, which while not necessarily immediately relevant to the con- cerns of the consultation nonetheless influence it, sometimes profoundly. To be complete, a diagnosis should be based on an appraisal of both levels of the clinical transaction (Balint 1964).

At this deeper level the clinical transaction is constituted by the often covert emotional and psychological contact be- tween patient and doctor. It is the product of the interaction of their individual personalities within a particular context. The degree and quality of personal contact must be sufficient to sustain the clinical work of the transaction. One of the doctor's tasks, therefore, is to try to ensure that the clinical transaction proceeds with public and personal levels in harmony. Beyond a certain point, discord between patient and doctor means that desired outcomes of the consultation may be jeopardised. It will become clear that the counselling skills intrinsic to being a doctor (here termed 'intrinsic counselling skills') are those neces- sary for the effective monitoring of the equilibrium between the two levels.

Parting company

Apart from the giving of advice, the etymology of counselling reveals that the word also means 'to go together' (Oxford English Dictionary). With many patients in everyday clinical practice it is so. Regardless of the nature of the patient's ailment or its sever- ity, there is a spirit of collaboration, of going along together. Each party performs an appropriate, often reciprocal, role (as doctor or patient) following a more or less mutually agreed pathway leading to the achievement of therapeutic goals.

Doctor and patient going together does not, however, imply that their clinical encounter is an easy-going affair. Indeed, it may be arduous. Painful, embarrassing or frightening condi- tions can impose considerable demands on doctor and patient as they pursue their roles within the clinical transaction. When there is a parting of the ways this can sometimes be obvious and the resulting clinical transaction becomes unsatisfactory to both patient and doctor. At other times, doctors may continue as if going along with their patients, only later to discover that they had never been on the same track or, indeed, had been proceeding in completely different directions! The time spent in the company of the patient may be satisfying to the doctor, even though stated goals are not achieved. This is especially likely when doctor and patient become friends. The main, if not the stated, purpose of the consultation can then become social rather than clinical, with the result that important clinical concerns may be neglected. Within such transactions, which appear on the surface to progress smoothly, the parting of the ways is more subtle but still requires the doctor's formal attention.

Public and personal levels

In any clinical transaction doctors need to be able to recognize **departures** – the signs which indicate a parting of the ways – whether or not these are obvious. They must then decide how to intervene in order to get back together with the patient. As emphasized above, such getting together with the patient relates to two levels of interaction. The more obvious is the **public level** of their interaction and the more covert and idiosyncratic is the **personal level**. Doctor and patient can be together at one level but not at the other. Successful consulting depends upon at least a degree of togetherness at both the public and personal level of interaction with the patient.

Each level, public and personal, potentially affects the other in a multiplicity of ways. An initial, single departure at either level of interaction can affect the other level and may be enough to uncouple the mutual efforts of doctor and patient in dealing with the problems in hand. Furthermore, a departure by patient or doctor can induce a similar, a complementary, or a completely unexpected departure in the other. Such departures can be subtle, sudden and quite often happen unawares. The result is a clinical transaction which is far from straightforward in terms of the roles taken and the goals striven for. The doctor may be baffled by the ensuing interpersonal situation and sometimes bewildered by the speed of transformation of an apparently straightforward clinical transaction into one that has become puzzlingly complicated.

Mr Morton

*At 19, Danny Morton had suffered from diabetes mellitus
for ten years. The management of his disorder, for the
previous year, had been problematic. Difficulties associated
with re-establishing control over blood sugar levels, however,
were coped with relatively smoothly since Danny enjoyed
a supportive relationship with the elderly consultant
paediatrician to whom he had been referred many years before
and who had continued with his care past the usual age of
handover to adult services. The consultant then retired.*

*Referral to the adult services brought a different
consultant and a different approach. The new consultant
believed there was more than a hint that Danny was
deliberately manipulating his insulin dosage in a dangerous
and self-destructive manner. The new consultant's consulting
style was active and challenging compared to that of Danny's
former consultant. Towards the end of the first consultation,
after the consultant had suggested there was little he could do
if Danny did not comply fully with advice, Danny became
verbally abusive and physically threatening. The police were
called to remove him from the outpatient department.*

Mrs Bradley

*Mrs Bradley had been given much dietary advice and taken
a range of remedies from her family doctor for her irritable
bowel syndrome. Ultimately, all proved unhelpful even though
each new approach was accompanied by a transient
symptomatic improvement. Mrs Bradley would return to her
doctor recounting the return of her symptoms in great detail.
However, she studiously avoided blaming her doctor for her
lack of improvement. Instead she seemed to show much
sympathy and warmth towards her, as if feeling sorry for
someone who had tried so hard and yet achieved so little.*

*In the presence of this patient the doctor felt
comfortable. Only after a consultation was over did she
fleetingly feel otherwise – impotent and angry. She would then
feel somewhat guilty at harbouring such negative thoughts
towards Mrs Bradley, who was, to her mind, so long-suffering
and grateful. It took a long time for the family doctor to
question her own relatively positive disposition towards this*

patient whose potentially treatable condition was not really improving.

While few would disagree that the clinical transaction involving Danny was far from straightforward, formulating a shared understanding of how and why the transaction had gone astray is more difficult. The situation with Mrs Bradley is even harder to understand. The departures here are subtle and agreement as to how they might be construed still less likely. In both cases, however, most would agree that the clinical transactions had gone sufficiently off course to mean that desirable clinical goals were not achieved. Certain aspects of the interaction of patient and doctor had resulted in significant departures from the straightforward pursuit of these goals.

With Danny, the focus of the clinical work was lost ostensibly because of the unhelpful influence and interference of aspects of the personal level of the interaction with his new consultant. With Mrs Bradley there was no obvious disruption at either the public or personal level of the interaction with her doctor. The two signs that the transaction was not as straightforward as it seemed were that her condition was not responding to advice or treatment and that the doctor felt unduly positive during the transaction, especially given that the patient was getting no better.

Whether departures are gross or subtle, however, it is important to recognize that something untoward has gone on and to try and understand why. To this end it is helpful to have a schema to apply to clinical transactions which can facilitate the identification of deviations from the straightforward path. This is the first step to both patient and doctor getting back on track.

The clinical transaction

We are now in a position to put forward a more formal model of the clinical transaction. As we have suggested (see also Norton and Smith 1994), such a model helps to identify how and why transactions go awry and may indicate areas for appropriate intervention. In many instances problems arise because the personal level of interaction does not support the work at the public level.

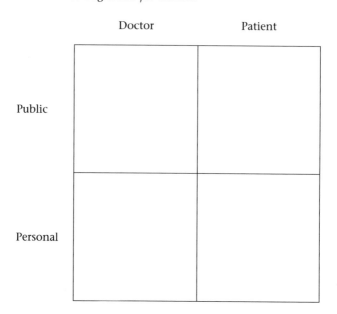

Figure 2.1 The transaction window

Within the clinical transaction, therefore, the doctor's intrinsic counselling skills are directed towards ensuring that problems at this level are avoided or rectified and not ignored or minimized.

The **clinical transaction** between doctor and patient can be defined as *an appropriately negotiated, goal-oriented interaction between doctor and patient, comprising both public and personal components* (Norton and Smith 1994). Although the criteria for this definition may not apply to all clinical transactions (for example in some medical emergencies where the patient is unconscious or psychotic), such a definition is applicable to a wide range of clinical encounters in family and hospital practice. Described in this way, the clinical transaction can be pictured as a four-celled matrix (like the four-paned Johari's window) divided horizontally into public and personal levels, with the vertical division separating doctor and the patient, as shown in Figure 2.1. We call this matrix the **transaction window**.

The public interaction with the patient, which comprises much of the overt clinical work, involves establishing a common language. It relies on the doctor's ordinary social skills and,

Table 2.1 Preconditions or stages required for straightforward clinical transactions

---

 1 The patient seeks appropriate health care based on
 2 an accurate self-perception of illness and/or symptoms and
 3 trust in the doctor, which leads to
 4 a timely presentation to a doctor who is
 5 suitably trained, and
 6 well disposed towards the patient, and thus
 7 able to diagnose accurately any medical disorder and
 8 deliver (or refer for) appropriate treatment, advice, reassurance, information or explanation, leading to
 9 acceptance of the same by the patient, who
10 within the expected time returns to a state of health or acceptable level of adjustment to any continuing illness.

---

more specifically, the consulting skills discussed in Chapter 1. For perhaps the majority of the millions of clinical transactions that occur daily within health services, the doctor and patient are likely to understand one another sufficiently so that information is adequately imparted by and to the patient, even if painful and emotional aspects are also present.

But as we have seen with the cases of Danny and Mrs Bradley, clinical transactions are not always straightforward. Here we define a **straightforward clinical transaction** as one in which, *as far as is appropriate, clinical goals are negotiated and a management strategy agreed which is conscientiously pursued by doctor and patient until a mutually acceptable termination (or agreement not to terminate) is achieved.* By contrast, a **complicated clinical transaction** represents a transaction in which there is *a significant, non-transient departure(s) from the straightforward clinical transaction, at the public or personal level, or both* (Norton and Smith 1994).

Even a straightforward clinical transaction demands that a complex set of criteria are met, comprising public and personal level elements, which have implications (including responsibilities) for both doctor and patient (Table 2.1). Doctor and patient are helped by the social construction of their respective roles. Expectations of each other, and the skills and attitudes needed, are both formally (as via the doctor's training) and informally acquired. Doctors are assumed to have the necessary knowledge and skills and are expected to remain 'professional' whatever the clinical situation. But the patient's role is also demanding and requires a sufficient degree of sophistication and accomplishment in terms of personal integration and adaptive social and psychological functioning. Doctors must remain cognizant of the potential effects of illness itself, as well as of personality and wider transcultural differences.

Public level departures

For the patient, common departures involving public level aspects include an inaccurate evaluation of symptoms and, as was suspected of Danny, failure to comply with treatment or advice. Patients often overestimate the significance of symptoms but can underestimate them too. They may incorrectly ascribe causes, and also anticipate solutions to their symptoms, which affect how they elect to present them. According to the degree of anxiety attached, or the extent to which their normal coping strategies are overstretched, the presentation might be inappropriately premature and urgent on the one hand or dangerously delayed on the other. On the doctor's side, departures in the public domain may be the result of failures of training or of continuing professional development, and diagnostic or management errors, any of which may lead to an inability to deliver appropriate treatment, explanation or advice.

Personal level departures

For the patient's part, departures from a straightforward clinical transaction at the personal level may have their origins in a range of thoughts and feelings and be manifest in attitudes and behaviours reflecting a basic mistrust in or inappropriate respect for the doctor. Problems of low self-esteem may lead to difficulties in asking for and receiving help. The doctor too may not be well-disposed towards the patient. Various labels are used by doctors to refer to patients whom they experience as problems – hateful, fat-folder, heartsink (Groves 1978; Schrire 1986; O'Dowd

1988) – and patients may refer to their doctors as quacks or butchers or by other unflattering epithets. Alternatively, either doctor or patient may feel unusually positive towards the other, as was the case with Mrs Bradley and her doctor. How doctor and patient relate beyond the constraints of their social roles, how they react to each other as people, depends on their individual personalities. A full exploration of the important and complex issue of how humans relate to one another is clearly beyond the scope of this book.

Interactive effect of departures

Departures at either level are likely to impinge on the process of the clinical transaction. A single departure at one level, if un-attended to, may have a knock-on and complicating effect at the other level (Figure 2.2). A patient's failure of trust at the personal level, for example, may affect public level compliance with

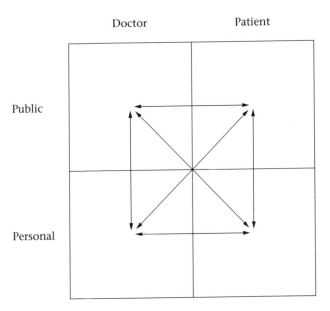

Figure 2.2   The transaction window: possible interactions

treatment. Alternatively, misdiagnosis or incorrect or unsuccessful treatment may lead to a failure of trust. Once mistrust has become established, tracking down the original departure is difficult since interactive effects may serve to compound the situation, obscuring its origin within the clinical transaction. The consequence may be to provide still more work for the doctor in trying to disentangle and understand just what has gone on.

Expressed in these terms, a two-level model of the clinical transaction not only illuminates the complexity of the interactive situation between patient and doctor but also can help reveal the origin of any departures which may have arisen during its process. Construing clinical transactions in this way can help the doctor in the task of monitoring potential partings of the way – indicators of *not* going together.

Transaction windows

The transaction window facilitates a view of the clinical transaction, albeit a snapshot, which can help the doctor organize information about such problematic situations. The preconditions for a straightforward clinical transaction can each be assigned to one of the four cells of the matrix as shown in Figure 2.3. Using this as a template, any departures from a straightforward transaction, once noticed, can also be assigned a place. Although this may not show exactly where or why the departure initially occurred, it provides a convenient tool with which to hypothesize and explore how the current situation may have arisen. It can also help the doctor hypothesize and experiment with a range of possible responses or interventions and gauge their likely effectiveness.

Such a conception of a clinical transaction is, of course an abstraction, and cannot do full justice to all the shades and nuances of the doctor–patient interaction and their effects on the outcome of the transaction. Nor do we recommend that doctors necessarily construct transaction windows with pen and paper, although this can be useful as a teaching or discussion aid, to which we return below and in Chapter 8. With experience, a mental review of a complicated transaction along the above lines can facilitate a productive response.

	Doctor	Patient

Public	5 suitably trained
	7 able to diagnose
	    accurately
	8 able to deliver
	    appropriate treatment,
	    advice or explanation
		1 seeks appropriate health
		    care
		2 accurate self-perception
		    of symptoms
		4 timely presentation
		9 accepts treatment,
		    advice or explanation
		10 regains health

Personal	6 well disposed towards patient	3 trusts doctor

Figure 2.3   The transaction window
The conditions for a straightforward transaction allocated to
the 'panes' of the window

Danny

*To the surprise of the diabetologist, Danny kept the next
appointment following his ignominious removal from the
outpatient clinic. In the mean time, the consultant had given
thought to what had happened at their last clinical encounter.
He believed he had been over-zealous in challenging Danny's
behaviour so soon in this new transaction and also insensitive
in not mentioning the loss of the former consultant to whom
Danny might have been understandably attached.*

*Thinking about their altercation and its possible causes,
the consultant toyed with the idea of giving Danny a chance
to explain why the previous management of his diabetes had
worked so well for so long. Using the transaction window, he
sketched some possible scenarios and anticipated that such a
public level intervention might be well received and could
improve their interaction at the personal level (Figure 2.4).*

*After the two had exchanged wary looks, the consultant
put his plan into action. He acknowledged he might have been*

too challenging and that Danny might be missing his old consultant and wondered what had worked so well in the past. To his relief Danny readily acquiesced to this new approach. He seemed eager to talk about missing his old consultant but was also prepared to embrace a more adult relationship with the new one.

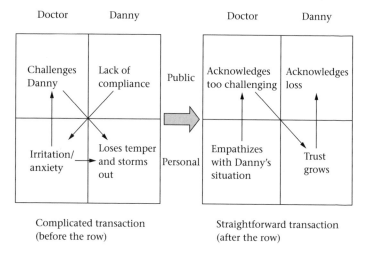

Figure 2.4   Transaction windows sketched by Danny's doctor

As in this case, some departures are readily understood and reasonably easy to remedy. Nevertheless it required the doctor to reflect on his own and Danny's behaviour, to put himself in Danny's shoes and try to see things from his perspective. An empathic, even if retrospective, appreciation of Danny's loss of the older consultant and the challenge of the new situation, allowed the doctor to interpret this to Danny, who then had a chance to express his feelings. With the help of the transaction window, by making time for a little more talking, and using facilitative and linking responses (see pp. 17–19), Danny's new consultant made good use of both intrinsic and general counselling skills. That he did so was in this case perhaps of crucial importance for the continued well-being of a patient with a serious long-term disease.

Other complicated transactions require more thought and attention on the part of the doctor but can equally repay this effort. By so doing, doctors may well be able to prevent progression to further complications which might result in a complete breakdown of treatment, or seriously jeopardize the doctor–patient relationship in other ways.

Mrs Bradley

Having come to the conclusion, somewhat counter-intuitively, that it might be questionable to feel so positive in the company of a patient who was faring so poorly, Mrs Bradley's family doctor began to think about repeating patterns within their transaction. Mrs Bradley was now a regular weekly attender and occupied an appointment slot at the end of every Friday evening's list. At a time when most people wanted to have the working week behind them, Mrs Bradley appeared content to rehearse her latest week's worth of woeful bowel symptoms.

Having constructed a transaction window of the clinical transaction with Mrs Bradley, the doctor pondered her own positive feeling. The longer she thought, the less reason she saw for feeling so sympathetic. She now began to feel more assertive and no longer so guilty about her feelings of frustration which emanated from a sense of therapeutic impotence (Figure 2.5).

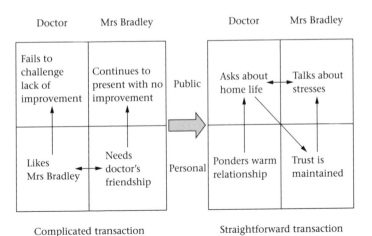

Figure 2.5 Transaction windows sketched by Mrs Bradley's doctor

> *At their next meeting, in spite of its time in the week,*
> *the doctor enquired in detail into Mrs Bradley's life outside the*
> *surgery and away from her routine complaints. As a result she*
> *uncovered a long-standing marital problem and a host of other*
> *family and business difficulties and worries. In terms of*
> *stressors, weekends were little different from the rest of the*
> *week for Mrs Bradley. She had virtually no respite from the*
> *various stresses in her life, save for the weekly 'session' with*
> *her doctor. As she considered this, her doctor felt annoyance*
> *tinged with sadness. Later, she referred Mrs Bradley to the*
> *practice counsellor and eventually the latter was enabled to*
> *make changes to both her work and family situation,*
> *incidentally with a beneficial effect on her bowels. The visits*
> *to her doctor were reduced to three-monthly.*

Mrs Bradley's doctor became aware of the contradictions that
had been established in her interaction with Mrs Bradley. She
had responded warmly to the attractive and lively personality
that her patient presented and was gratified by the respect and
appreciation that Mrs Bradley evinced. Yet she was eventually able
to acknowledge the ambivalent and frustrated feelings which
arose because whatever she prescribed, Mrs Bradley did not get
better and because she seemed quietly to have come to regard
occupying the last appointment on Friday as almost her right.
Using the transaction window helped the doctor clarify her awareness that the transaction with Mrs Bradley had become complicated – the failure of her clinical efforts became obvious. She
wondered about her own positive feeling towards this patient
and questioned whether it was this that Mrs Bradley so lacked
from others in her life. This led to her decision to explore the
patient's personal situation more deeply, which turned out to be
time well spent in the effort to break the therapeutic stalemate.

The ability to reflect upon one's own feelings and to understand the part they play in maintaining a complicated clinical
transaction can be a difficult skill to acquire. The process of
acquisition can be greatly facilitated by reviewing such transactions with peers, and especially with trained and skilled super-
visers. Once acquired, such awareness can be put to profitable
use, as we saw with Mrs Bradley. It also allowed Mrs Bradley's
doctor to appreciate what might be missing in Mrs Bradley's life

and prompted her to explore this more openly. This brought the patient's personal needs, stresses and anxieties into the public domain where they could be 'treated' alongside her bowel symptoms in a more productive way and with Mrs Bradley's more active participation.

Conclusions

In this chapter we have advanced a model of the clinical transaction as a complex interaction between doctor and patient that proceeds simultaneously on two levels – public and personal. Within the public level interaction, both parties pursue the goals of the transaction, adopting relatively well-defined roles. In order for the public level transaction to proceed smoothly, however, the personal level of interaction must be sufficiently harmonious.

For a clinical transaction to be straightforward it must meet a number of conditions. Familiarity with these alerts doctors to any departure from them which may lead to the transaction becoming complicated. The two-level model of the clinical transaction emphasizes the complexity of the potential interactions between doctor and patient. This is diagrammatically represented by the transaction window. The model takes account of the fact that although a complication may become manifest as a departure in one cell of the matrix, its cause may have arisen in another. Viewing the clinical transaction with the aid of the transaction window can help doctors to discover where and how things have gone awry.

Applying this model of the clinical transaction entails paying close attention to the equilibrium between the doctor's own public and personal domains. Checking the elements present at the public level is relatively easy and routine, for instance retaking a history and reviewing a diagnosis or the response to treatment. A less familiar task is looking for and acknowledging evidence of any out-of-the-ordinary reactions or feelings towards the patient, whether positive or negative.

The ability to form a picture in the mind's eye of the overall progress of a clinical transaction and the interactive elements of which it is comprised, including a critical appraisal of the doctor's own part in it, is an important intrinsic counselling skill. It is a skill which can be developed and enhanced through training and can make a literally vital difference on occasion. The application of the clinical transaction model provides doctors with a structured way of monitoring the clinical transaction. As we shall see in the following chapters, applying the model helps doctors at each stage in the clinical transaction to identify, avoid or rectify any complications which might otherwise threaten desired clinical outcomes.

Chapter 3

Making a diagnosis: the history

We are, in an important sense, the stories of our lives. How sickness affects us depends on how sickness alters those stories. Both sick persons and physicians make the experience of sickness more meaningful (thereby reducing suffering) by placing it within the context of a meaningful story. Physicians, because of their special knowledge and their social role, have special powers to construct stories and to persuade others that these stories are the *true* stories of the illness.

(Howard Brody 1987: 182)

Introduction

Narratives about patients and their illnesses form a legitimate part of the exchange of knowledge and ideas among doctors (MacNaughton 1995). A well-chosen case vignette places the hard data of medical statistics within a human context. From the patient's perspective, however, illnesses are events, usually unwelcome and sometimes alarming, within the ongoing story of their personal lives. When making a diagnosis this context cannot be ignored, although it may be emphasized to a greater or lesser extent, depending on the clinical setting and the urgency of the problem. A diagnosis is therefore much more than the name of a disease; to be complete it should be given in terms of its physical, psychological and social impact.

All the consulting skills we have so far discussed will be needed as doctors elicit information from patients in order to make a diagnosis and put this information to work for the patient's benefit. Although it cannot always be assumed, the active cooperation of patients, and often of their family too, is essential. As we saw in Chapter 2, doctor and patient ideally work together at both public and personal levels of the clinical transaction. Doctors do have power and expertise but, if they are to keep public and personal levels in harmony, they need to be wary of using their authority simply to persuade patients that the medical account of their history is the true one. Care must be taken that the patient's assumptions, hopes, fears and expectations are properly understood. The doctor's own assumptions should not exclude patients from full participation because the latter do not hold them in common or understand them (Nettleton 1995).

As throughout this book, our intention in this chapter is to concentrate on the two levels of engagement of doctor and patient, public and personal, and on how they interact within the clinical transaction. As we have seen, intrinsic counselling skills are deployed to monitor both levels of the transaction for evidence of any departure from the straightforward. This involves paying particular attention to any untoward shift in the equilibrium between public and personal levels which might be sufficient to disrupt the collaborative clinical work of the transaction.

The diagnostic process

There are distinguishable phases in the process of making a diagnosis. These need not necessarily be consecutive but can overlap or recur as the transaction progresses, and may be omitted altogether (Byrne and Long 1976). The usual sequence is for history-taking to be followed by a physical examination of the patient. Any abnormal findings may then be explained and a provisional diagnosis discussed, before further investigations are arranged should these be needed to confirm the diagnosis. In each of these phases of the diagnostic process the relationship between patient and doctor is somewhat different. During a well-taken history there should be some sense of collaboration between equals. Submitting to and performing an examination, however, is tangibly different and necessarily a more unequal event (see Chapter 4).

Once the physical examination is completed a sense of equality may be at least temporarily re-established while findings are discussed and any necessary investigations proposed. The patient may then need to submit once more, however, this time to possibly painful, frightening and invasive investigations, some or all of which the doctor may need to do personally. A difference in the gender of patient and doctor will have implications throughout the diagnostic process, particularly so when the history and subsequent examination involves sexual or other intimate problems.

Both doctor and patient, therefore, will anticipate and experience each phase of the diagnostic process with a range of personal attitudes, expectations and feelings. As we shall see, it is important that doctors are aware of this and, as far as possible, remain in touch with such aspects of themselves and their patients. This is particularly true of those occasions where the diagnosis is serious or life-threatening or when the true diagnosis is masked by other aspects of the patient's account or how it is presented. The transitions from phase to phase of the diagnostic process must be sensitively managed. The model of the clinical transaction we have outlined (together with the use of the transaction window) helps the doctor preserve a functional and constructive equilibrium between public and personal domains as the history unfolds.

Taking a history

When it comes to making a diagnosis nothing is more important than a good clinical history (Fraser 1987). Many factors are involved including the setting, the greeting, seating arrangements, body language, active listening, the appropriate use of silence, the use of open and closed questions and many other aspects of the medical interview, including how the personalities of doctor and patient combine (Balint 1964; Pendleton *et al.* 1984; Fraser 1987; Norton and Smith 1994). Any or all of these factors may have an impact on doctor, patient or both and, through interactive processes, influence both public and personal levels of the clinical transaction. While pursuing the clinical history, therefore, the doctor must engage in the additional task of continually scanning the transaction at both levels for any signs of departure from the straightforward.

There are several obstacles to obtaining a good clinical history. Many patients would find it hard to provide a complete account of their problems, even if given an attentive ear, without skilful prompting by their doctors. There is no formal training for the patient role and patients may not be sure what aspects to include or what might be of relevance to the doctor (Armstrong 1986; Nettleton 1995). They may be embarrassed or ashamed, fearful of revealing their symptoms and attendant anxieties, or they may minimize symptoms because they dread the intimate examination which might follow. Some patients are easily put off by an abrupt or uninterested manner, insensitive probing or too much medical jargon. Patients who are reticent or inarticulate in voicing their expectations of and hopes for the clinical transaction can make it difficult for their doctors to obtain an adequate history.

The history can also be obscured by other factors. These include the tendency of some patients to present emotional problems as somatic complaints or even to present fictitious illnesses for ulterior motives. Patients with certain personality disorders or psychiatric illnesses may also have particular difficulty in giving a history. If so, the process of history-taking is made correspondingly more arduous (although not deliberately so) for their doctors (Norton and Smith 1994). Especially problematic are presentations which lack appropriate emphasis or emotional content. In such circumstances the doctor may be tempted to disregard or minimize the complaint or even to regard it as counterfeit.

Illness inevitably has its impact within the personal domain, an impact which can affect the doctor as well as the patient. The doctor may need to address directly a patient's emotional response (or lack of it) by making it part of the public domain work. Acknowledging fear and uncertainty, incapacity and loss, or disgust and threats to self-image can be important aspects of managing illness. For the most part, however, in respect of their professional role, doctors must restrain their personal reactions to the patient's illness, particularly as the history of that illness first emerges. This effort of restraint can sometimes be burdensome and isolating. It is therefore of great value if doctors, especially during training but also throughout their careers, are able to discuss particularly upsetting cases with colleagues or supervisors.

The depth, breadth and focus of the history of a patient's illness varies to some extent depending on the context. Histories differ in emphasis and detail depending on whether they are taken by a family doctor in a GP surgery, a consultant gynaeco-logist in an outpatient clinic, or by a harassed junior doctor in a hectic Accident and Emergency Department. In general practice particularly, several problems may be presented within a single interview, and the problem of most importance to the patient may not be the first to emerge. This aspect of the history may well be the most difficult to talk about, and to listen to. It may not be offered at all if the earlier and 'easier' problems are not dealt with sensitively enough. History-taking is necessarily selec-tive, especially in emergency situations, but the above possibili-ties should always be borne in mind.

The process of history-taking does more than furnish the pieces of a diagnostic puzzle. It establishes a relationship between the patient and the doctor, the quality of which has very prac-tical implications. If it succeeds in fostering a relationship of mutual cooperation and understanding then it is more likely to support doctor and patient as they pursue and complete a plan of management. In some circumstances this relationship may be extremely brief offering little if any scope for reparation if things go wrong. Consider, for instance, the relationship of anaesthetists to their patients. In other circumstances it can develop and last for many years, as is commonplace in family practice.

Mr Nelson

Mr Nelson was 54. He had worked all his adult life as a scrap metal dealer. Having married late, he and his wife still had three children at home. They had recently moved and registered with a local general practice. As a young man, Mr Nelson had had surgery for a prolapsed disc and, although he now had little in the way of sciatica, the pain and limitation of movement when bending and lifting was making work impossible. He had seen medical specialists, physiotherapists and osteopaths, and knew there was little that could be done to improve his condition. He attended surgery that morning hoping to be given a sick note. Indeed, having taken a seat at the doctor's invitation, he opened with this request. The doctor was aware of a feeling of weary irritation.

He took care to conceal this, however, simply asking what the problem was and then listening for almost two minutes as most of the above history emerged. Contrary to his initial scepticism, it convinced him that Mr Nelson had a genuine problem. As the history unfolded the doctor became more relaxed and attentive but Mr Nelson appeared a little tense and anxious throughout.

Miss Conrad

Sophie Conrad was 17. At the start of her final year at school she had become unwell, tired all the time, with little energy for her usual active pursuits. After initial investigations had turned out to be normal and yet Sophie still showed no signs of improving, her GP had mentioned that she might be suffering from 'ME' (myalgic encephalomyelitis). Mrs Conrad, who always attended with her daughter, was concerned by the possibility of this diagnosis and asked for Sophie to be referred for a specialist medical opinion. This her GP did. Sophie returned with her mother soon after, both very upset. The specialist they had seen had asked them who had made such a diagnosis. After a brief examination, he had gone on to say that he believed there was no such condition as ME. Sophie was probably suffering anxiety because of her forthcoming A levels. A second specialist opinion was requested to which the GP acquiesced. This time Sophie and her mother seemed happier. Although no definite diagnosis had been made, they reported that the specialist had listened to them carefully and taken Sophie's complaint seriously. Over the next several weeks, Sophie did in fact return to her customary good health – the episode of illness remaining unexplained.

In the case of Mr Nelson the doctor was aware of his immediate negative reactions but was also able to contain and not reveal them. He had jumped to the conclusion that he was about to be drawn into a difficult negotiation and was being asked to certify what he suspected might prove to be a spurious incapacity to work. His initial feelings, therefore, represented a departure from his usual well-disposed attitude, i.e. a departure from the straightforward clinical transaction. Had the doctor acted in response to his immediate feelings then the clinical transaction would almost certainly have become complicated. By opting to listen rather than react the doctor avoided this danger. After allowing time for the complete history to emerge uninterrupted, his negative feelings had been mostly dispelled. Listening also allowed the doctor time to reflect usefully on his feelings, as we shall see later.

The case of Sophie Conrad involved a series of clinical transactions. That with the first specialist was manifestly complicated. Sophie's mother had been particularly upset by the contemptuous tone the specialist had adopted and was visibly distressed as she reported it to the GP. Unlike Mr Nelson's GP, as the history of suspected ME was revealed, the specialist had apparently made no effort to conceal his negative feelings or gauge the likely effect on Sophie and her mother. That the second specialist consultation had been much more acceptable to them, even though no diagnosis had been made, testifies to the importance of listening to the patient's story carefully and respectfully. Both the above clinical examples illustrate the importance of preserving the equilibrium between public and personal levels of the clinical transaction.

The public–personal equilibrium

Under normal circumstances, most patients and doctors perform their respective roles within the clinical transaction with the equilibrium between their own public and personal levels maintained within a range which permits them to pursue the clinical transaction straightforwardly. In other words, they are able to remain sufficiently in touch with their own and each other's feelings about what is happening for the transaction to be appropriately meaningful but without being overwhelmed by those feelings. The balance between public and personal elements is set within a characteristic range for each individual and reflects the style with which a person habitually interacts with others (Norton and McGauley 1998). For example, those for whom public level aspects predominate may appear very task-oriented, matter-of-fact and businesslike and display little evidence of emotion. Conversely, those for whom the equilibrium is tilted towards personal level aspects may appear to be always anxious, suspicious or to wear their hearts on their sleeves.

When doctor and patient meet in the clinical transaction, therefore, there may be some need for mutual adjustment should their interactive styles be uncongenial. For instance, some doctors find it hard to tolerate anxious patients or those who readily become tearful. If so, they need to be particularly vigilant when consulting with such patients for any indication of departure from the straightforward transaction. For their part, many patients find clinical transactions unsatisfactory where the doctor is focused solely on the clinical task and gives them no signs of being emotionally in touch. It is also the doctor's responsibility to bear this possibility in mind. Provided that the interaction between doctor and patient does not stretch either's functional equilibrium beyond its limits, however, the transaction is likely to proceed straightforwardly. In such circumstances, doctor and patient establish a shared, interactive equilibrium for the clinical transaction as a whole which is capable of sustaining the clinical work. This is what we mean by doctor and patient going along together.

The range within which the public–personal equilibrium remains functional for each individual is determined by a number of factors. Some of them are relatively fixed and depend on aspects of personality, including a person's psychological mechanisms of defence against anxiety (see Chapter 9). For the doctor's part, such aspects are influenced by professional training which helps doctors tolerate relatively high levels of anxiety (and other emotions) when faced with certain diseases or emergency situations or when dealing with certain types of patients.

Patients have no such training and therefore may need to rely on the doctor's ability to assist them to maintain a functional public–personal equilibrium. This is especially true if the problem is frightening, debilitating or its management demanding. Gauging the state of this equilibrium within the clinical transaction and maintaining it within functional limits call on the doctor's intrinsic counselling skills. This means that doctors must remain alert to signs of any disturbance of the equilibrium in themselves or in their patients and for signs of interactive effects which might threaten a harmonious relationship between the two.

Transference and countertransference

The influence of past or contemporary relationships, such as in the family or peer and work groups, affect doctor and patient alike. Deprivation or abuse during upbringing, for example, can significantly affect a patient's ability to trust the doctor, to ask for or receive help and hence to provide a straightforward account when giving a history (Norton and Smith 1994). Submitting to an examination may similarly be made more difficult. The influence of such external relationships is often described in terms of the psychoanalytic notions of transference and countertransference. A brief account of these processes is therefore relevant here.

The process of transference affects everyone to some degree. Its effect is to cast the present interpersonal engagement within the terms of past formative relationships, usually because certain, sometimes only very superficial, similarities obtain between the two situations. This means that patients may relate to doctors as if they are relating to another person or situation influential in their past. If these modes of relating have been difficult, dependent, destructive or dysfunctional in other ways then, to the extent that they are re-enacted within the clinical transaction, they pose a threat to its straightforward progress.

Transference in the clinical transaction is, at least initially, an unconscious process. Doctors, therefore, can find themselves cast in the role of some figure in the patient's past, often an authority figure. Unwittingly, they may then react to that patient as if they were taking on aspects of that role. This is part of what is meant by the term countertransference. Thus, the personal level of the clinical transaction, together with associated expectations which affect the transaction at both levels, can be influenced by relationships which are external to the clinical transaction itself. Furthermore, these relationships may well belong to the distant past.

If the straightforward progress of the clinical transaction appears to be disturbed by processes of transference imported into it by the patient, these may be usefully explored as the history progresses. At the beginning of this chapter we emphasized the importance of rendering a complete diagnosis in physical, psychological and social terms. This means taking full account of relevant elements at both levels of the clinical transaction. A detailed psychosocial enquiry, which can be a routine part of history-taking, may well illuminate the origin of these disturbing influences and allow them to be brought into the public domain. Doctors must take care to minimize any risks to the straightforward clinical transaction deriving from their counter-transference reactions to patients.

Mr Andrews

Mr Andrews, a large and heavily tattooed young man, opened the consultation with an orthopaedic surgeon with a request for relief of the pain in his shoulder. He seemed suspicious of and reluctant to answer the surgeon's routine questions. After some minutes of heavy-going conversation, the surgeon said, in a friendly tone, 'You don't like answering questions, do you?' Mr Andrews replied that he did not see the point; all he wanted was some effective treatment. The surgeon then explained that if he was going to do anything to help he needed to be sure it was the correct treatment for the condition. Mr Andrews seemed to accept this, grudgingly, and was more forthcoming.

Mr Andrews had spent some time in a young offenders' unit and regarded men in positions of authority with some suspicion. He had had a particularly stormy relationship with his own father and, via a process of transference, he unwittingly anticipated that the orthopaedic surgeon would be similarly antagonistic and unhelpful (see also the case of Danny).

Mr Nelson

After examining Mr Nelson (see page 41), an examination which supported the history of his back problem, the doctor decided to question him further. He had noted Mr Nelson's air of tension and his own initial feeling of weariness which had not quite lifted even though the irritation had gone. He suggested to Mr Nelson that this back condition must be worrying and depressing. Mr Nelson readily agreed. He went on to say that he was experiencing serious financial difficulties and that he had become very depressed.

During this clinical transaction Mr Nelson's GP experienced a range of feelings. His initial sceptical reaction cast Mr Nelson in the role of other patients in the doctor's experience who had asked him for what he felt was unjustifiable sick certification. The countertransference reaction of irritation was characterisitic of this doctor in situations where he was being asked to do something he thought was wrong. Later on in the transaction, after this feeling had been dispelled, the persisting feeling of weariness became noticeable. This the doctor correctly construed as an empathic countertransference response to Mr Nelson's depression which he was then able to enquire about openly.

Professional detachment

At any stage of the clinical transaction, but particularly during history-taking, being aware that the attitudes or emotions that patients display when consulting may derive from past problematic relationships can provide doctors with extra room for manoeuvre. They can afford to feel less personally implicated and consequently less threatened in terms of their own public–personal equilibrium. Patients who are angry, distressed or dissatisfied may not be solely or even primarily angry, upset or unhappy with the doctor. Indeed, an awareness of this possibility contributes to what is commonly called professional detachment.

In terms of our model of the clinical transaction, we construe professional detachment as the doctor's ability to preserve a functional public–personal equilibrium even when in the grip of powerful emotions. Nonetheless, a functional equilibrium also depends on the ability of doctors to remain empathically in touch with their patients and to foster an interpersonal relationship that supports the clinical work of the transaction. To do so doctors need to remain alert to visual and other non-verbal clues that indicate what the patient may be feeling, as well as to their own emotional responses. It can be easy for doctors to become completely emotionally dislocated from their patients, especially from those who have difficulty revealing their emotions and expressing them directly.

Immediate and overt reaction to these emotions, whether sympathetic or antagonistic, may not serve the overall aims of the clinical transaction best. Yet they can serve as a guide to the doctor's responses or interventions in the public domain.

As we have described above, in Mr Nelson's case the doctor's persistent feeling of weariness had been a clue to the existence of Mr Nelson's depression. The doctor was able to return to this aspect of the history after his examination had confirmed Mr Nelson's back problem.

Conclusions

History-taking is the most important of the phases of the diagnostic process in so far as it affords the first opportunity to forge a positive working relationship with the patient. In so doing, it paves the way for subsequent phases of the clinical transaction which might otherwise be more awkward or distressing. It is an opportunity for doctor and patient to affirm expectations of each other, concomitant with their respective roles, and to develop a common language in which to frame an account of the patient's presented problem. As the history unfolds there should be an appropriate balance between public and personal levels of the clinical transaction – a functional public–personal equilibrium.

The ability to monitor and gauge this equilibrium, so as to be able to intervene to explore and restore it if necessary, is an intrinsic counselling skill of the medical consultation. As such, it helps the doctor decide on the nature and timing of active responses, as well as highlighting the need to contain and restrain emotional responses to the patient rather than to react unthinkingly. The effective use of intrinsic counselling skills, therefore, enhances appropriate professional detachment and, at the same time, allows doctors to remain in empathic contact with their patients.

To the extent that they make use of intrinsic counselling skills, doctors are more alert to their patients' attitudes and feelings and their own in response. Any such feelings, on either side, together with attitudes and behaviours, may originate in or be influenced by past or present relationships outside the clinical transaction. If so, they may well seem out of place in the context of the clinical transaction and it may be pertinent for the doctor to try to discover whence they originated. If on the doctor's side, then steps should be taken to exclude them from the clinical transaction, usually without involving the patient. If they seem to originate in the patient then it may be helpful to address them within the public domain, for example by including a detailed psychosocial enquiry in the history.

The history of a patient's illness is rarely complete, however rigorously taken. New aspects tend to emerge throughout the clinical transaction and doctors should remain alert for unexplored but relevant issues which might surface. As far as they can, they should try to avoid foreclosing the history by making assumptions about the patients' understanding of medical problems or contributing to a relationship which does not support an open and honest interchange.

Chapter 4

Making a diagnosis: examination and investigation

> Once the patient is undressed, exposed and lying down, the imbalance of power is further accentuated. In what other interaction, apart from another very ancient one, can a professional say to a client 'all right, stop talking and take your clothes off'?
>
> (David Metcalfe 1989: 221)

Introduction

In most medical textbooks the physical examination of the patient is presented as the second phase in making a diagnosis. It follows history-taking as an appropriate continuation of the problem-solving process, which may already have included a more or less formal examination of the patient's mental state and social circumstances. During history-taking the relationship between patient and doctor takes on a certain character and tone which in each particular instance is more or less conducive to the straightforward progress of the clinical transaction. To this extent it sets the stage for any subsequent physical contact. Patients usually expect to undergo physical examination during a consultation and indeed satisfaction with the consultation as a whole is often increased if an examination is included (Kravitz *et al.* 1996). As with any phase of the clinical transaction, however, the examination has its impact on the equilibrium between public and personal levels of the doctor–patient interaction, an impact accentuated by the 'imbalance of power' (Metcalfe 1989).

Many professional groups, such as lawyers, social workers, counsellors and psychotherapists, develop intimate relationships with their clients. Unlike doctors, however, one thing they are not required to do is physically examine their clients. Intrinsic counselling skills, with which to monitor the public–personal equilibrium, are as important for doctors during the physical examination, as they are when taking a history. If anything, as we shall argue, they become more important. Going along with the patient, mediated in the process of history-taking by words and silences, has now to be sustained during physical contact which can vary from the apparently trivial to the extreme. In this respect, it should be borne in mind that what may seem trivial to the doctor, part of a well-practised routine, may be experienced by the patient as something much more significant. An ability to monitor and preserve the appropriate balance and harmony between public and personal domains therefore remains crucial to the success of this phase of the diagnostic process.

Touch

During the course of a clinical transaction doctors may use any or all of their senses to help them arrive at a complete diagnosis of the patient's problem. Sight, hearing, smell, even taste – testing for the saltiness of cystic fibrosis – and especially touch are all capable of providing valuable evidence to support a clinical diagnosis (Asher 1972). As well as being a vehicle for eliciting information, touch is also a particularly powerful medium of non-verbal communication. However intimate or searching history-taking may have been, examining and being examined bring new elements to the clinical transaction, mediated by the anticipation of and response to touching and being touched. Touch is part of everyone's daily existence and there are many personal, social and cultural barriers and taboos that relate to physical contact of various sorts (Argyle 1988). In a medical setting the physical examination of patients of necessity often transgresses these boundaries.

During this phase of the clinical transaction patients are liable to be at their most passive and the balance of power at its most unequal. How patient and doctor individually cope with this situation will depend on many factors. Both will have been prepared to a greater or lesser extent by their training or experience in the roles of doctor or patient respectively. Clinical detachment is part of the doctor's professional role. This depends, as we saw in Chapter 3, on the doctor's capacity to sustain an appropriate equilibrium between public and personal aspects of the clinical transaction. The ability to do so may be further tested when physically examining a patient. Doctors may have to struggle, for example, with some degree of anxiety due to fear of inflicting pain or have to tolerate other emotions such as embarrassment or shame, either in themselves or in their patients. After all, patients may be asked to expose parts of their bodies to a tactile exploration they have never experienced before.

Touching and being touched raise issues of power and submissiveness as well as of gender and sexuality and therefore have profound resonance within the personal domain. The intimacy of a physical examination may be even greater than that permitted in other social or family contexts, between parent and child or sexual partners. In terms of the required submissiveness of the patient, it may reawaken emotional traces of a powerlessness not experienced so strongly since babyhood. Such rekindled and potentially disturbing feelings, even if repressed and so kept out of consciousness, are still capable of influencing the doctor–patient interaction.

An individual's experience of being physically examined is inevitably also coloured by the nature of physical handling received from carers in the formative years of childhood, as well as by previous experiences of being a patient. Although guided by clinical concerns, the way in which a doctor approaches and probes the patient's body, whether roughly or gently, confidently or hesitantly, will depend on similar formative influences. Such factors, especially if amplified by the doctor–patient interaction, can sometimes evoke emotions powerful enough to erupt into the public domain making examination difficult, even traumatic, for both patient and doctor.

Samantha

Samantha, a shy 10-year-old, attended the Paediatric Clinic having been referred by her GP because of recurrent abdominal pains. The young male senior house officer (SHO), after taking the history from Samantha and her mother, then tried to examine her abdomen. Samantha, however, drew up her knees and giggled at the first touch. The doctor laughed and asked if

*she liked being tickled. After this inappropriate comment it
became impossible for him to examine her properly and the
attempts to do so finally led to tears.*

Samantha was showing the first signs of puberty. She considered
being tickled undignified now that she was 10. The only tickling
she permitted at home was from her brother. He was two years
older and they quite often engaged in protracted, although not
overtly sexualized, rough-and-tumbles in which being tickled
played a major part. The doctor, for his part, felt much more comfortable with babies and younger children and lacked confidence
when he approached Samantha.

In such a situation it is particularly important that the doctor
remains alert to the equilibrium between personal and public
levels of the interaction and that appropriate boundaries are
maintained. Within any clinical transaction issues of sexuality
may be heightened via skin-to-skin contact or if the examination requires the exposure and manipulation of sexual organs or
areas of the body associated with sexual arousal. Patients who
have experienced sexual abuse in childhood are likely to find
cooperating with such physical examination particularly problematic. Furthermore, if there has been oral abuse, examination
of the mouth, especially with a spatula or endoscope, may prove
as emotionally difficult as genital or rectal examination. If the
interaction between patient and doctor becomes sexualized it can
lead to inappropriate touching or exaggerated responses to being
touched. These in turn can result in complications of the clinical
transaction that amount to gross professional misconduct and
the abuse of the patient or to false accusations of such.

Expressive and instrumental touch

Words can be used either expressively, conveying terms of endear-
ment and other emotions, or instrumentally, as when questioning
or instructing someone in order to gain information or control
behaviour. In many cases the distinction between these different uses is not easy. Ultimately, expressive language is offered
to another unconditionally whereas instrumental language is
imposed and, if it is not to be coercive, requires collaboration

and consent. A similar distinction can be applied to different sorts of touch (Morris 1964). Within the public domain, an instrumental approach is both a necessary and expected part of the clinical work. At a personal level expressive touch, such as a hand laid on a forearm or a pat on the shoulder, helps unite doctor and patient in their shared humanity. It rescues the patient from becoming a mere object and the doctor from becoming an unfeeling machine. Both sorts of touch, therefore, can be important during the clinical transaction.

To touch or not to touch, however, can be a controversial subject. During history-taking expressive touch may help to foster a bond of trust and greater openness between doctor and patient. It can therefore be used alongside verbal interventions to establish and preserve an appropriate public–personal equilibrium within the clinical transaction. But care must be taken when using expressive touch and helpful guidelines have been suggested. Accordingly, four factors should be considered:

- clarity regarding boundaries
- congruence of touch
- the [patient's] perception of being in control of the physical contact
- the [patient's] perception that touching was for their own benefit rather than the therapist's.

(Horton *et al.* 1995)

When it comes to the physical examination, touching is unavoidable and, as part of the diagnostic process, instrumental touch is necessary. The doctor's hand is a knowing hand which expects to find evidence for or against the clinical hypotheses formulated during history-taking. Touching in this sense is an activity which is based firmly in the public domain, at least as far as the doctor is concerned. Nevertheless, there will inevitably be powerful effects at the personal level. In cases of skin disease or infection there may be feelings of disgust. During intimate examinations, such as rectal or pelvic examination, there may be embarrassment, distaste or the inappropriate intrusion of sexual thoughts and feelings. Other emotions can also intrude. For example, doctors may feel intimidated by the fear of finding something which suggests very serious disease, such as a malignant lump. On the other hand, they may feel triumph at discovering evidence for a favoured diagnosis. Such feelings, if communicated, may well seem inappropriate to the patient.

Doctors, as individuals, will vary in terms of how and to what degree they are affected by touching patients during a physical examination. Emotional reactions, arising in the personal domain, however, must be monitored and may need to be contained rather than admitted into the interaction with the patient, if complications are to be avoided. Through their training and experience most doctors will be able to sustain an appropriate public–personal equilibrium and to use a correspondingly appropriate combination of expressive and instrumental touch. To an extent, however, this will depend on patients also being able to perform an appropriate and reciprocal role.

As well as the risks associated with the transgression of boundaries discussed above, the potential clinical usefulness of an examination may also be diminished through other effects of the interaction between doctor and patient during the examination. An overanxious or cautious doctor, for instance, may fail to probe deeply enough when examining an oversensitive patient. Alternatively, an insensitive doctor may inhibit an otherwise cooperative patient from relaxing sufficiently by probing more forcefully as the patient contracts or withdraws rather than pausing and proceeding more gently.

The experience of being examined

As we have already emphasized, touch is a powerful medium of communication. The way a doctor examines a patient, reacts to touch and to what the touch reveals, and the doctor's responsiveness to the patient's reaction, all communicate something to the patient. The use of expressive touch, a comforting hand on the shoulder or the holding of a hand, counterbalances the necessarily impersonal and inquisitive probing of the instrumental examining hand. The whole experience of the examination, of course, is influenced by the quality of the doctor–patient relationship that has already been established. The professional and interpersonal boundaries, implicitly or explicitly embraced before the examination, have now to be maintained as the examination is carried out. This may be particularly difficult during intimate examinations. Ideally, therefore, while performing an examination, doctors should try to remain aware of what the experience might be like for the patient.

Intimate examination

Most patients, when asked, say that the intimacy of oral, vaginal or rectal examination is something that has to be tolerated as a necessary part of the clinical transaction (Larsen *et al.* 1997). Attitudes towards such examinations, and the strategies employed to cope with feelings that such examinations evoke, vary with the individual patient but will also depend in part on the interaction with the particular examining doctor. In a study of women's attitudes to intimate examination before, during and after childbirth, women described several coping strategies (Weaver 1997). 'Deflection', for example, meant concentrating on the idea of purpose or function to avoid dealing with any sexual connotation that the exposure and examination of genitals might have. Childbirth was taken to be a physical function, and those in attendance were acceptable provided their presence had a function in the birth. 'Distancing' involved women in separating themselves off mentally from what was happening to their bodies. 'Rationalization', the most commonly deployed coping strategy, involved a reasoning process which rendered the examination less embarrassing. It tended to be used where women felt their medical carers were in empathic contact.

The coping strategies outlined above helped women patients in clinical situations where the equilibrium between public and personal levels is particularly prone to being disturbed. Concentrating on the public level tasks and the reasons for them helps to support a functional equilibrium. Childbirth, however, is a good example of a clinical situation where the acceptable range of this equilibrium, for patients as well as professionals, is expanded to accommodate much more expression of personal level elements. This also applies to aspects of the care of terminally ill patients. In circumstances such as these doctors themselves often adopt similar coping strategies in order to retain their professional role.

When it comes to the gender of the examining doctor, somewhat surprisingly, patients state that they have no strong preference (Heaton and Marquez 1990). Given a choice, most men and women opt for a doctor of the same gender but some women prefer pelvic examination to be done by a male doctor, feeling less embarrassed and believing that a man would be gentler (Roberts 1985). Such studies are inconclusive but the issue of gender is an important one. Suffice it to say, doctors should be alert to gender issues as possible complicating factors in the clinical transaction, at any stage, but especially when intimate examinations are involved.

Mrs Jackson

Mrs Jackson wished to consult her GP about bleeding after sexual intercourse. Anything to do with her sexual life, including any associated smells or soiling, were matters of extreme embarrassment to her. She had great difficulty in providing her doctor with a complete history and became extremely agitated when a vaginal examination was proposed. The doctor openly acknowledged this difficulty explaining that this was a routine aspect of her work in such cases and that she would proceed as considerately as possible. She added that Mrs Jackson could call a halt or pause in the examination at any time. Allowing her to undress behind the curtains the doctor proceeded slowly and gently, merely laying her ungloved hand on Mrs Jackson's knee for a moment when Mrs Jackson became too tense and waiting until she could relax again.

The Royal College of Obstetricians and Gynaecologists (RCOG) have published guidelines for doctors performing vaginal and pelvic examination, many of which can be applied to examinations in general. They recommend that:

- careful consideration should be given to the necessity of the examination
- the reason for the examination and what it involves should be explained
- the patient's permission should be obtained
- a chaperone should be offered to all patients undergoing intimate examination, irrespective of the gender of the doctor

- private, warm and comfortable changing facilities should be available
- there should be no unreasonable delay before examination
- such examinations should take place in a closed room, without interruption from other people, bleeps or telephones, etc.
- the doctor should remain alert to all verbal and non-verbal signs of distress, and discontinue the examination when requested.

(RCOG 1997)

In addition: the examination, while thorough, should be as gentle as clinical necessity allows; personal comments should be avoided but relevant discussion and questions encouraged; full explanation and discussion of the clinical findings should be delayed until the patient is dressed and seated once more (Barclay 1998). It will be readily appreciated that following these guidelines contributes to the maintenance of the public–personal equilibrium and so helps minimize the risk of departure from a straightforward clinical transaction.

Further investigation

Much of the discussion above concerning physical examination applies to any further investigation the patient may have to undergo. Patients may have particular anxieties about needles, X-rays or other 'high-tech' machinery. Such concerns can be addressed before patients are exposed to them and the experience also discussed afterwards, if need be. In most cases they should be told what will happen and what it is hoped or feared any investigation might reveal. Patients have little control over this phase of the clinical transaction and will be helped to cope the more they understand of its purpose and what it will entail.

Further investigation of the patient is often carried out by doctors or medical professionals other than the doctor who initially took the history and performed the examination and, furthermore, at a different time and place. It may thus hold new anxieties for patients, in terms of dealing with the unfamiliar, and mean waiting (sometimes considerable periods) for appointments and results. It also means that referring doctors may have little or no control over an important phase of the clinical transaction.

Doctors may not themselves be completely familiar with what certain specialized investigations entail and so be unable to prepare their patients. However, the onus is on them, rather than the patient, to find out.

The patient becomes involved in a different system of health care provision when referred for investigation. Patients inevitably, therefore, carry both public and personal level residues from the clinical transaction into this system and bring new issues back to it. These may have to be specifically addressed when the clinical transaction resumes, quite apart from the public level information that the investigations have contributed. For example, if patients experience an investigation as much more traumatic than they were lead to believe, this may become an issue requiring attention in its own right.

Mrs Edwards

Mrs Edwards had been referred by her GP to the Radiology Department at the local hospital with a request that they carry out a barium meal examination for a suspected peptic ulcer. It was the hospital's customary policy to perform an endoscopic examination in these situations rather than a barium meal. The radiologist performing the examination told Mrs Edwards this and asked her to mention it when she returned to her GP. He had himself discussed the matter with the GP on more than one occasion.

Mrs Edwards found the barium examination extremely unpleasant and vomited several times afterwards. She attended the surgery to hear the results with mixed feelings. She felt an uncomfortable obligation to pass on the message from the radiologist and at the same time was left wondering if she had been properly investigated. She also felt the need to report how ill the examination had made her feel. Somewhat fortunately, the referring doctor was on holiday and she saw another partner at the practice with whom she felt able to discuss all these concerns.

Doctors also interact with the systems to which they have referred their patients for investigation, as Mrs Edwards's case illustrates. They not only have professional relationships with the members of these other systems, but also may have relationships which have a significant impact at the personal level. Such pre-existing relationships, although external to the ongoing clinical transaction with the patient, nevertheless have the potential to influence it, as happened in Mrs Edwards's case. Here, the GP who had referred Mrs Edwards for her barium meal was embroiled in a strong professional disagreement with the radiologist who performed it. This disagreement disturbed the radiologist's public–personal equilibrium to the extent that he unprofessionally involved Mrs Edwards in the dispute.

The pre-existing relationship between Mrs Edwards's GP and the radiologist had a significant impact on Mrs Edwards, both in terms of her relationship with the radiologist and the relationship with her general practitioners. Doctors, therefore, must take on the additional task when monitoring the clinical transaction, of gauging the potential influence of the quality of their own relationships with the professionals in other health systems to which patients are referred. Usually relationships in and between such systems operate harmoniously in the interests of the patient but some attention should be paid to ensure that this is, in fact, the case.

Conclusions

Intrinsic counselling skills can and should be applied to the clinical examination as much as to the taking of a history. Their use must embrace an awareness of the imbalance of power which is at its most extreme during this phase of the diagnostic process. Consequently, doctors should remain alert to the effect this has on themselves as well as their patients. Power must not be abused. Doctor and patient continue to interact during the physical examination, although few words may be spoken. Certain physical examinations are particularly likely to raise issues of gender and sexuality.

What happens during physical examination has significance at both public and personal levels and, as with all phases of the clinical transaction, the interaction must be monitored for possible departures from the straightforward wherever these may originate. As always the endeavour should be to maintain an appropriate equilibrium between public and personal levels.

Any interventions should be aimed at preserving or restoring this equilibrium. In respect of the powerful impact that physical and especially intimate examination exerts at the personal level, guidelines for examining patients are recommended which reinforce the public level interaction. Further investigation of the patient may necessitate the involvement of other medical professionals and an interruption in the clinical transaction. The patient may well be exposed to painful or frightening procedures with which the doctor is not always fully conversant. Patients can be better prepared for such investigation if the need for it is explained and accurate information given about what to expect.

The involvement of other systems of health care adds an extra dimension to the doctor's task of monitoring the clinical transaction for evidence of complicating effects. Doctors are already familiar with taking into account the influences of family and other social groups on patients and how this can affect both public and personal levels of interaction within the clinical transaction. They should anticipate that the process of investigation will also have an impact on the patient, over and above the public level implications of any resulting clinical information, and that this may require attention when the patient returns. Assessing the effects of their own professional relationships on those whom they refer for further investigation is not a familiar task for most doctors. This matter is explored fully in Chapter 7.

Chapter 5

Managing the problem

> Just as one shouldn't try to heal the eyes without the head, or
> the head without the body, so one shouldn't try to heal the body
> without the soul either; and this is the reason why so many disesaes
> baffle doctors – because they ignore the whole, which they ought to
> take care of, since if the whole is not well, it is impossible for part
> of it to be so.
>
> (Plato 1987: 181)

Introduction

After arriving at a diagnosis of the patient's problem, the main
function of the clinical transaction becomes the management of
that problem. How this is achieved depends upon many factors,
for example, the nature of the disorder, its treatment, the complexity of the clinical tasks and the personalities of both patient
and doctor. In some transactions the patient presents a discrete
problem which is treatable by a single particular medical or surgical intervention. Other situations, however, are more complex
since they involve chronic conditions or long-term treatment
which requires that patients forgo aspects of their usual lifestyle
such as smoking, drinking alcohol and eating unhealthily (see
Chapter 6).

 With the exception of certain emergency or other unusual
clinical situations, sharing diagnostic information with the patient
is desirable, so that an appropriate plan of clinical management
can be discussed and agreed. The patient is thus enabled, whenever possible, to make informed decisions concerning their future
welfare. Such an approach requires that the possible side-effects
or other risks associated with the treatment are carefully considered and evaluated with the patient. Ensuring that patients

fully understand such information, however, allowing for cultural differences, legal rights and taking into account mental state as well as any particular difficulties in learning ability, may pose a problem, not least because it can be time-consuming.

Notwithstanding any such obstacles, crucial to the success of this endeavour is the doctor's careful monitoring of the equilibrium between public and personal levels within the clinical transaction – *not* 'separating the soul from the body' (Plato). This activity, the effective deployment of intrinsic counselling skills, complements and enhances the doctor's general communication skills that we discussed in Chapter 1. In this chapter we examine how intrinsic counselling translates into the everyday clinical tasks of informing patients of their diagnosis, fostering a therapeutic alliance and gaining consent for, and maximizing compliance with, treatment.

Imparting the diagnosis

Arriving at a diagnosis is the culmination of a collaborative endeavour between patient and doctor, sometimes involving other professionals if special investigations are needed. With the exception of large-scale screening of healthy individuals as part of health promotion programmes, the diagnostic process is usually initiated by the patient. Although patients may themselves have a more or less accurate theory about what is wrong, the clinical diagnosis is initially known only by the doctor. Linked with the diagnosis is knowledge concerning treatment and prognosis of which the patient is also likely to be initially unaware. The doctor faces the task, therefore, of imparting the diagnosis in such a way as to both inform the patient and also secure compliance with treatment, often thereby optimizing the prognosis. As we have seen, this endeavour entails the doctor making an effort to explore patients' understanding of the presented problem and their expectations of what is to follow.

When the diagnosed condition requires no active treatment or is easily treatable and the condition carries no social stigma, there is usually little difficulty. The public–personal equilibrium, for patient or doctor, is unlikely to veer off balance. The impact of the diagnosis at the personal level, even though it may provoke emotions such fear, disgust, disapproval or shame, is not sufficient to interfere with the collaborative effort needed at the public level to manage the problem. If, on the other hand, the disease is untreatable or socially stigmatized (for example, sexually-transmitted diseases or certain parasitic infestations) or the treatment is demanding of the patient, then the task of fully imparting the diagnosis can be difficult. In such cases doctor, patient or both may be so affected at the personal level that they are unable to engage fully with the demanded public level tasks.

Denial

In the above situation it is especially important for the doctor to be confident in having the relevant skills to impart diagnostic information so as to ensure it is fully understood by the patient. This means adequately communicating with the patient not only at the public level of their interaction (avoiding jargon, etc.) but also at the personal level. Through empathic responses and an accurate assessment and reflection of the patient's feelings, the doctor seeks to ensure that the personal level communication with the patient is consonant with that at the public level.

Imparting 'bad news' concerning a diagnosis can be particularly difficult (Buckman 1994). In such cases the clinical information may be met by denial or other rebuttal. Depending on the individual characteristics of the patient, the necessary balance between public and personal levels may be tipped one way or another. If the equilibrium is sufficiently disturbed, the patient may either be overwhelmed by emotion or, alternatively, seem to accept rationally at the public level what they have been told without registering its significance emotionally. Doctors need, therefore, to be aware of the public–personal *dis*equilibrium that this represents and the reasons for it, if the quality of communication necessary for the management of the problem is to be achieved.

Patients who 'deny' tend to tax their doctor's tolerance and are consequently notoriously hard to manage – one variety of so-called 'heartsink' patients (O'Dowd 1988). The concept of denial in relation to medical illness, however, is not clear-cut.

Denial may be in relation to the illness itself or to its implications, such as lifestyle changes required for its successful management. Distinguishing so-called 'healthy' denial from 'pathological' denial is also an important task for the doctor, since for some conditions a degree of denial may be associated with a better prognosis. For instance, in the face of life-threatening or terminal illness, denial of the fullest implications of the diagnosis may allow patients to function more normally and cooperate more wholeheartedly with treatment (Morley 1997).

In some clinical transactions factors operating within the doctor contribute importantly to the patient's denial. In such instances, doctors may not be sufficiently in touch with their own personal level feelings and reactions. As a consequence, information imparted to the patient may be communicated in a mechanical way, devoid of appropriate empathy. The patient's response may then be, perhaps unsurprisingly, similarly lacking in appropriate emotion. It is as if doctor and patient only go through the motions of agreeing a plan of managment, but the patient's subsequent compliance with treatment and adaptation to the illness at a personal level is impaired. Furthermore, the supportive relationship between patient and doctor is likely to be undermined.

In other instances, personal level factors in the doctor, rather than being appropriately contained, surface to complicate the public level transaction. Patients may then find themselves having to deal with obvious distress or other emotions in their doctors. This can happen, for example, when doctors are good friends with their patients or are unduly sensitive to the anxiety or suffering that a diagnosis implies. In the face of certain diseases, they may betray feelings of anxiety, disapproval or disgust. Alternatively, the doctor's personal reaction to the diagnosis may lead to the problem being minimized or evidence for it ignored. Here, as in the first instance above, it may be the doctor's denial, rather than the patient's, which complicates the clinical transaction. Illness in the doctor or the effects of too much stress or tiredness may also contribute to a loss of the doctor's ability to maintain an appropriate balance between public and personal levels within the clinical transaction. Importantly, they also make it less likely that evidence of the patient's denial will be observed, evaluated and adequately dealt with.

Dr Jones

Dr Jones had known his patient for as long as he had been a partner in his general practice. The two were old friends – ever since Dr Jones had diagnosed his patient's atypical appendicitis. The patient's admiration for Dr Jones had deepened over the years as they found themselves playing a range of sports together. This relationship was one of equals and only fleetingly had either considered whether their professional relationship, as doctor and patient, was inappropriate.

One day his friend discussed with Dr Jones, informally and half-apologetically, that he had been suffering from rectal bleeding. Dr Jones good-humouredly suggested that just as the patient's 'acute abdomen' had almost certainly been appendicitis, this bleeding was 'probably piles' and almost certainly benign. The matter was taken no further at that time. The bleeding did not stop, however, and it was nine months later when Dr Jones's friend made an appointment with the GP registrar in the practice. On this occasion a rectal examination revealed what turned out to be an inoperable rectal carcinoma.

In this example it was the doctor's inability to entertain a 'negative' diagnosis in a longstanding friend which led to the patient not taking his own health concerns seriously and so delaying re-presentation for a medical opinion with such a tragic result.

Denial of the implications of the diagnosis

Even though patients may understand the serious significance of their diagnosis, and react with appropriate emotion, the longer-term implications may not be fully appreciated or acted upon.

Mr Lewis

At 54, Mr Lewis had considered himself a fit man until he was admitted to hospital with chest pain. Tests revealed that he had quite extensive ischaemic heart disease. He accepted this diagnosis without any indication of appropriate concern,

even though he had been involved in a discussion of his
smoking and dietary habits and lack of significant physical
exercise. Over the next few weeks he was noted by his friends
to be more irritable than usual. He continued to smoke and
did not modify his diet or increase his exercise in spite of the
efforts and exhortations of his wife and GP.

In Mr Lewis's case, his denial of the implications of the diagnosis
took some time to reveal itself. He had intellectually accepted
the diagnostic information but, aside from being more irritable,
he did not seem able to register or process his emotional reaction to it, with the result that he failed to make important lifestyle changes. Impediments to change, including denial, should
always be anticipated and, if necessary, taken into account (see
also Chapter 6). A full psychosocial enquiry may reveal aspects
of a patient's psychological make-up, life and circumstances which
suggest that such difficulties may be likely. In turn, some of these
may need to be brought to the public domain in order to help
resolve them.

Doctors are not equally adept at dealing with all illnesses
or all of their implications and not equally at home with every
type of patient. Failure in the public domain, due to lack of
knowledge, experience or competence in dealing with an illness,
may mean that information necessary for the patient's full
involvement in treatment is not forthcoming. Such failures may
be unacknowledged or minimized by the doctor. They may be
compounded if doctor and patient do not get on. The result is
that even the most expert and specialized of doctors have some
appropriately referred patients who take them to the limits of
their expertise and technique. Failure to recognize when this
occurs may mean that, for their own personal reasons, doctors
in such a situation are unable to communicate information or
discuss a diagnosis with their usual professional composure and
public–personal equilibrium.

Mrs Brown
It was the ward sister and house surgeon who returned after
the ward round to discuss the diagnosis with Mrs Brown.
Histological findings revealed a carcinoma of the breast for
which a mastectomy had been carried out. The consultant

surgeon had dwelt on the practical issues of wound healing and drainage and had been pleased that the pathology had appeared to be local and totally resected. Perhaps his relative pleasure in this and his patient's good physical progress meant that he was oblivious to Mrs Brown's remaining unease. This was manifest in a stunned silence during which she had no questions to ask him. The surgeon had taken her silence on the matter to indicate that she had no lingering problems of any kind – relating to body or soul. It was left to the ward sister and house surgeon to help Mrs Brown cope with her emotional reaction to the diagnosis, a task they accepted as an unwritten part of their job descriptions.

Doctors, especially in hospitals, are likely to work in collaboration with others as part of a multidisciplinary team. In some circumstances the presence of colleagues serves a complementary role and can make up for any important omissions, as with Mrs Brown. Other doctors or nurses in the team, for example, may be well placed to observe the clinical transaction and signs of public–personal disequilibrium and, potentially, be better placed to deal with it. Within a team, however, it may also be possible to draw the team's attention to unacknowledged omissions or failures at public or personal levels. The need for further training or greater sensitivity may thus be highlighted (see Chapters 7 and 8).

Fostering a therapeutic alliance and compliance with treatment

Ideally, any professional endeavour is underpinned by an interpersonal relationship which incorporates mutual trust and respect. In practice, there are many times when this ideal is not achieved. Often, minor departures from the ideal interpersonal relationship are of little or no lasting significance. In some instances, however, departures do matter. When they do, they may be obvious and immediate in their effect, such as when open hostility (as with Danny and his doctor) or even violence erupts. Alternatively, they may be hard to detect and only insidiously incremental in their overall complicating effect. In the context of some long-term doctor–patient relationships, it may be safe to assume that adequate trust and respect exists. Each party may have been 'tried and tested' over a number of years. Trust and respect, however, are not all-or-nothing, once-and-for-all attributes and it is prudent for doctors not to take such aspects for granted.

Some patients have had more than their fair share of illness and adversity. Because such aspects tend to coexist, patients so affected can have particular difficulty in maintaining any trusting and respectful relationships, including those with doctors. Often they may have had little or no experience of trust and respect during their formative years. Among these patients are those who comply least well with treatment. They suffer further, therefore, on account of their own mistrustful personalities. If they can neither form a therapeutic alliance nor comply with treatment, any diagnosis or condition of which they are informed tends to be associated with a worse prognosis (Norton 1996).

A weak therapeutic alliance undermines all treatment, from the surgical to the psychotherapeutic. Doctors need, therefore, to be able to identify when a consultation or clinical transaction either is failing to achieve its goals or is not being pursued in an acceptably straightforward manner or both. The clinical transaction model and its associated use of intrinsic counselling skills helps doctors to recognize departures and to understand them in the context of a particular clinical transaction and the parts doctor and patient play in their production.

There are many potential reasons for, and routes taken by, departures from the straightforward clinical transaction. In practice, however, they often share a common basis. First, patients may have pre-existing, inappropriate expectations of doctors and the treatment they offer because of the quality of formative relationships with parents or other important care-givers and the effect this has had on the development of their personalities. Second, current factors relating to the actual diagnosis and its treatment or to the interaction of particular personalities may be influential. The result, however, may be that initial departures interact to become amplified and impair the development of trust and respect. Such was the case during Danny's first encounter with the new diabetologist (see pp. 24–5).

Whatever the reasons for departures from the straightforward clinical transaction, once recognized, they need to be rectified if doctors are to continue to help their patients. Doctors, for their part, must keep in mind the potential effect on the clinical transaction of a mismatch of personalities or consulting styles between themselves and their patients. Although doctors may well find these attributes hard to alter, they are open, to some extent, to the influence of training and enhanced self-awareness. Other efforts centre on educating patients as to how to perform their role as patients appropriately and focusing on the establishment of clear and negotiated goals for the clinical transaction. This can include setting appropriate limits to expectations and behaviour and dealing with issues surrounding the endings of clinical transactions or the termination of treatment episodes.

Clarification of the patient's role

The patient's role is not learned in the same way as the doctor's professional role. If a clinical transaction is to proceed straightforwardly, however, patients must, within limits, perform their role appropriately (see Chapter 2). This role, manifest as 'illness behaviour' (Mechanic 1962), is informally acquired through the influence of the patient's immediate family and also the wider social network, including reporting of medical matters by the media. The result is that patients may vary considerably in how successfully they are able to fulfil the patient role. They may have unrealistic expectations of the clinical transaction in terms of what the doctor or broader health services can provide. Alternatively, their associated attitudes and behaviour may not be conducive to the doctor delivering what is, in fact, potentially available.

Doctors should not, and indeed cannot, legislate precisely what the patient's role should be. The roles of doctor and patient are liable to change as society evolves. Nonetheless, doctors may still need to educate patients about the appropriate presentation of their illness and what is required of both parties if the clinical transaction is to proceed successfully towards appropriate goals. It is important, therefore, for the doctor to openly and directly explore the patient's health beliefs and attitudes as part of the public level clinical work but remain alert to interpersonal aspects which may hamper that work. In this way, doctors aim to establish a mutual and reciprocal set of expectations with patients, consonant with respective roles, which can guide them as the clinical transaction is pursued.

Clarification of transaction goals

Sometimes the goals of the clinical transaction are not clear. This may be because there is no clear diagnosis or because the patient's presentation makes it difficult for the doctor to identify what precisely is the problem. Sometimes the patient may continue to attend or request appointments after the presenting problem has been resolved. Under these circumstances the doctor needs to clarify why the patient wishes to continue and try to identify any hidden, additional but relevant goals for the clinical transaction, for example, an undiagnosed depressive, anxiety or eating disorder. At some stage it may be important for doctors to state clearly those complaints which are relevant and those which are inappropriate. Obviously, in a specialist setting, appropriate problems and goals may be much more narrowly defined than in general practice.

When patients present with multiple problems or have multiple diagnoses, it is an important task for the doctor to decide on which to concentrate, particularly as consultation time is inevitably limited. Part of this task may include establishing that some problems are interlinked and can be addressed together. Sometimes patients experience questions directed at clarification as criticism or evidence of the doctor's mistrust. As always, therefore, it is important to monitor the personal level interaction throughout.

Some patients feel unable to disclose personal information because of a basic mistrust of professionals generally, due to low self-esteem or ambivalence about seeking help (Norton and McGauley 1998). It may be useful, therefore, to explain the importance of establishing an open dialogue and to indicate that reasons for reticence are appreciated. The doctor can also explain without criticizing the patient how mistrust, low self-esteem and ambivalence pose real obstacles to establishing an adequate therapeutic alliance.

In spite of careful explanations of this kind, some patients are not helped and merely feel patronized by the doctor. Under

such circumstances the doctor's attempts at education, a pre-
dominantly public level endeavour, have merely reinforced the
mistrust, low self-esteem or ambivalence. Such a response from
patients may have an impact on doctors at the personal level,
because all their best efforts seem to have been rejected. It is
important, therefore, for doctors to contain impatience or dis-
appointment and to try to avoid 'lectures'. Rather, they should
convey to patients, and accept themselves, the fact that developing an appropriate degree of mutual trust within the clinical transaction inevitably takes time. Such an approach may go some way
to keeping doctor and patient going along together, albeit sometimes at a considerable, although tolerable emotional distance.

Limit-setting and treatment contracts

Sometimes, even after roles and goals have been clarified and
re-negotiated, patients may behave in ways which make the
appropriate work of the clinical transaction impossible. In such
cases limits may need to be set as to what can realistically be
tolerated. Doctors may need to specify the lengths to which they
are prepared to go in order to try to help their patients. Sometimes it can be useful to reinforce such limit-setting by drawing
up a treatment contract. Such reasonable attempts by the doctor,
however, are not always gratefully received.

> *Miss Evans*
> *The Accident and Emergency consultant had been informed
> that his staff were extremely annoyed that a young woman
> was attending the department as an emergency on an almost
> daily basis. She presented in urinary retention and would end
> up by being catheterized. The medical and nursing staff were
> frustrated and angry, especially the female staff whose lot it
> was to carry out the catheterization. They felt that the patient
> was malingering and considered a punitive response would be
> useful. Consequently, on most occasions Miss Evans was kept
> waiting longer than necessary.*
>
> *The consultant's solution was to suggest that the patient
> should be taught to catheterize herself and be given a stock of
> catheters which she could collect from the department on a*

weekly basis. Miss Evans was informed of this apparently sensible proposal by a doctor who could not help but say it with a certain amount of triumphant relish. As a result the patient, who agreed to the plan, felt rejected. Although no longer in urinary retention, she continued to present daily to the department to catheterize herself as well as religiously collecting her weekly supply of catheters.

The use of even a simple treatment contract should not be entertained lightly, since there are many pitfalls that need to be avoided, as seen in Miss Evans's case. The most common is introducing the contract when either doctor or patient feel hostile towards one another. Under such circumstances no contract is likely to succeed (Miller 1989). The hostility which might have motivated the decision to implement the contract needs to subside to some extent and the public–personal equilibrium to be restored, before the contract can be satisfactorily negotiated.

Even introducing the idea of a treatment contract requires tact since it may be experienced by the patient as alienating or humiliating. The patient is likely to feel an unequal party in the negotiations, which merely serves to increase mistrust and disrespect. It is important that the conditions set are those which the patient can actually meet. If not, the contract is likely to break down, even if there has been initial agreement to it. If contractual conditions require patients to give up their only strategies for coping with intolerable feelings (for example, the use of illicit drugs or alcohol) and if no alternative coping strategy is offered or available to them, then the contract is also unlikely to succeed. Other professionals involved with the patient may need to be aware of the implications of any treatment contract for their own work with the patient. Sometimes the contract may inadvertently contradict the requirements or conditions of another approach, such as that of Probation or Social Services. Clearly this situation is to be avoided, if at all possible.

Terminating treatment

Often the ending of a consultation or treatment episode receives less attention than do the diagnostic and active treatment phases.

In many clinical transactions this poses few if any problems and the ending proceeds smoothly and satisfactorily. This is not always the case, however, and the conclusion of a transaction may be marred by many factors. These include the persistence of residual symptoms, the absence of a totally effective treatment or an inevitable worsening of a chronic condition. All of these may have consequences for the personal level of the doctor–patient interaction. Concluding a treatment episode may involve the patient in giving up the sick role, which because of changed psychosocial circumstances may have become difficult or un-attractive. In other instances, the patient, or the doctor for that matter, may have difficulties with endings of any kind. Such a difficulty, which stems from a variety of personal reasons, may become apparent only at the end of a clinical transaction which has been straightforward up to that point.

For many patients the changes associated with endings are emotionally charged because they revive echoes of past losses or endings that have been either unsatisfactory and/or incompletely accepted. This may mean that when doctor and patient have been brought into prolonged and intimate contact because of a particular illness and its management, the end of the treatment episode arouses emotions akin to those suffered in the past. The intensity and range of such emotions may seem inappropriate in the context of the clinical transaction.

Dr Owen

Dr Owen, a junior psychiatrist, was shocked when the middle-aged man whose depression he had apparently successfully treated as an outpatient broke down in tears at the suggestion that there was now no need for any further appointments. However, he recalled that this patient had had a brother who had died suddenly and unexpectedly when he was in his teens. Dr Owen was thus enabled to link the announcement of terminating the outpatient sessions with the death which had also came out of the blue. Making this link showed his appreciation of how shocking this might be for the patient. They consequently agreed to postpone the ending and meet for another three sessions. During these, the patient was able to talk in detail, and be in touch with much emotion, about the loss of his brother and what this had meant for him.

Discharge from a prolonged period of hospitalization may prove to be an event from which the patient never fully recovers emotionally, in spite of an apparent physical cure. Hospitalization due to psychiatric illness may be particularly likely to result in difficulty readjusting to the demands of everyday life in the wider community. It may be beneficial, therefore, for doctors to acknowledge and discuss the difficulties inherent in recovery from any period of hospitalization, as well as from the problems caused directly by the illness itself.

Where patients are particularly sensitized to issues concerning loss or separation, doctors need to take care to avoid inadvertently exacerbating their patients' problems. In primary care settings, when there is a question of referral for specialist advice and treatment, doctors need to be similarly sensitive. It may be important to take time to discuss such a course of action lest the patient experience the referral as both a loss and as a rejection. In respect of a psychiatric or other potentially stigmatizing referral, acknowledging that the limit of the doctor's expertise has been reached and that this is not a statement of personal dislike for the patient, as well as allowing sufficient time for the patient to understand this, may mean that the loss of the current professional relationship is more easily dealt with. Consequently the referral itself has a greater chance of being acceptable to the patient and having a successful outcome.

Doctors need to pay careful attention to endings, regardless of the length of a particular clinical transaction, even if of necessity endings have to be abrupt. Whenever possible, however, particularly in clinical transactions spanning several consultations, endings should be planned or negotiated together with the patient. This will help to ensure that the straightforward nature of the clinical transaction is safeguarded. Such an approach may prevent the patient from inappropriately presenting further complaints just before the end, in order to avoid the stress of the ending itself. An extra session or longer appointment to deal with leaving may be beneficial in the long run, if such time is used to deal with the issues surrounding termination. Allowing patients the opportunity to ventilate feelings of sadness and anger at the end of treatment may avoid further traumatizing those who are already particularly vulnerable to yet more unresolvable feelings of loss. Such feelings may well be expressed somatically, especially where residual symptoms persist or the illness is chronic or incurable.

Conclusions

The success of a clinical transaction is threatened by the influence of many factors. Some originate within the patient and others within the doctor but they may derive from adverse aspects of the doctor–patient relationship itself. While some transactions have become complicated long before a diagnosis is arrived at and discussed, fresh departures may be generated if the diagnosis is imparted inadequately or inappropriately. Faulty communication and counselling may place the therapeutic alliance at risk. If this alliance is impaired even eminently treatable conditions may not be successfully treated due to a failure of cooperation and compliance. Incurable conditions may rapidly deteriorate.

Faulty communication is particularly likely when public and personal levels of the interaction between doctors and patients are not in harmony. Doctors are helped in their professional role, therefore, if they are able to recognize when the public level clinical activity is out of phase with the interpersonal level and can learn ways of reconciling them. Ideally, the implications of diagnosis and treatment are adequately discussed so that patients are sufficiently informed to make sound and sensible judgements about their well-being. Communication is made more difficult when diagnoses bring stigma or the likelihood of disability, disfigurement or premature death. In such cases patients may deny the implications of the diagnosis, postponing or rejecting adequate discussion and negotiation of treatment or beneficial changes in lifestyle. This has the effect of uncoupling the interpersonal level of the clinical transaction from its public level task, making goals at the latter level much harder to achieve.

It is important that doctors remain alert to the various and sometimes subtle ways in which full and effective communication is blocked or avoided. They are helped by their understanding of the complex interaction which exists between the patient's personality, the illness and its treatment and the wider psychosocial environment. In addition, there is a contribution made by factors residing in doctors themselves, including their own personality, communication style and clinical competence. Recognizing all such aspects, and being able to ameliorate any adverse effect they may exert on the clinical transaction, represent important skills. Monitoring the clinical transaction for public or personal level departures and assessing the overall balance between public and personal levels helps to keep doctor and patient going along together.

Chapter 6

Health promotion

> The road to health promotion is not simply the exposition
> rationally of what it appears must be seen by all to be desirable. It
> involves understanding how and why both the 'lifestyle' and the
> 'health' of individuals are what they are, and the forces other than
> straight rationality that govern how successful people are in making
> changes – or, indeed, whether they even want to.
>
> (Eileen Cole 1990: 1)

Introduction

Thus far our attention has been on the interaction of doctor
and patient within a clinical transaction, in so far as this relates
to the diagnostic process, and the subsequent clinical management. We have emphasized that, at least initially, patient and
doctor may each have a different view and understanding of
the problem, illness or disease with which the patient presents.
Using those skills we have discussed, the doctor's task is to ensure that the understanding of the problem formulated during
the transaction is a shared one and that the clinical transaction proceeds straightforwardly. In most cases, there will be an
underlying assumption that the doctor has expert knowledge
of disease and its management of which the patient wishes to
take advantage. Usually, the threat of illness or disease, hover-
ing over the clinical transaction, provides considerable impetus
for doctor and patient to collaborate in achieving a successful
outcome.

Health is not simply the absence of disease and questions as
to how it is or should be defined and measured, and by whom,
are far from easily answered. Before doctors can engage in the task
of helping patients to maintain and improve their health, an

understanding of at least some of these issues is essential. Four dimensions of health can be distinguished:

- physiological fitness, based on objective measures
- disease, the medical dimension, on a scale running from no disease to the most serious and incapacitating
- illness, the subjective dimension, based simply on a symptom incidence measure
- psychological health, measured by feelings of stress and experience of symptoms of malaise.

(Blaxter 1990: 42)

Successful health promotion, therefore, is correspondingly hard to define and assess but the implications, both for the individual and for society, are far-reaching.

Within the privacy of the clinical transaction, exploring aspects of a patient's health and the behavioural changes that better health might entail, may call on all a doctor's interpersonal skills. Simply giving advice is unlikely to be effective. But matters of health are part of a very public arena in which many vested interests seek to express views and influence health beliefs, practices and health service provision. Community groups, women's groups, politicians, industry (food, nutrition, tobacco, alcohol, leisure), the media, as well as patients and doctors, all have ideas as to what is needed or desirable for better health. In so far as such vested interests constitute systems which overlap the clinical transaction (see Chapter 7), doctors must be mindful of their potential influence on the interaction with individual patients. Remaining alert to the impact of such factors on their patients and on themselves, at both public and personal levels, involves the intrinsic counselling skills emphasized in this chapter and throughout the book.

Social and individual perspectives

Since the mid-1970s, disease prevention and health promotion (perhaps two sides of the same coin) have taken centre stage in terms of the political and governmental agenda for health (Nettleton 1995). In the UK, both Labour and Conservative governments have produced White Papers emphasizing their importance (for example, *Prevention and Health* (Department of Health and Social Security (DHSS) 1977), *Promoting Better Health: the Government's Programme for Improving Primary Health Care* (DHSS 1987) and *The Health of the Nation* (Department of Health 1992)). The importance of health promotion is recognized worldwide and embodied in the 'Ottawa Charter' of 1986 (World Health Organization (WHO) 1986) and the 'Health for All by the year 2000' initiative. Accordingly, health is regarded as a right for all and should be viewed holistically. It is claimed to be too important to be left to medical practitioners alone and requires that inequalities between nations and social groups are eradicated (Tones 1997).

In the UK, the rise of the 'new public health' has inaugurated a shift in the emphasis of health concerns away from hospital based, high technology medicine, to community, public health and primary care initiatives. There has been a corresponding shift in attitudes, at least among some academics and policy makers, towards the view that health depends not so much on the diagnosis and treatment of disease by health professionals but on the lifestyles of individuals. Invoking individual responsibility for health has tended to overshadow even the well known social, environmental and economic causes of ill-health outlined so clearly in the Black Report (Townsend and Davidson 1982) and which was also addressed at the 1986 WHO conference in Ottawa.

Programmes of mass education, by government and other interested parties, seek to foster certain health beliefs and practices in a variety of ways. Increasingly, at least at governmental level, issues of economics and health rationing form a subtext to the altruistic goal of better health for all. Public health agencies seek to assess and address health needs and provide public information and services much more from the perspective of prevention and health promotion than in the past. It must be remembered, however, that set against this endeavour is the fact that health beliefs, in so far as they determine health-related behaviour, are diverse and do not necessarily correspond with the opinions of doctors or health policymakers. They may be idiosyncratic, familial or cultural, or representative of factions or interest groups. Health beliefs and practices and the efforts to promote health may not all be harmoniously directed towards the same goals.

The patient as customer

The shift in focus onto the patient, while also highlighting individual responsibility for health, has emphasized patients' rights and legitimate expectations of health services. There has been a shift from paternalism to consumerism. Within health service provision, consumerism has come to mean:

- the maximization of patient choice
- the provision of adequate information
- raising standards of health care
- shorter waiting times for treatment
- seeking and taking into account patients' views on services
- ensuring satisfaction and encouraging patients to complain if not satisfied.

(Nettleton 1995: 249)

This new emphasis on the patient as consumer is enshrined in *The Patient's Charter* (Department of Health 1991).

Such changes in policy and attitude have profound implications for the clinical transaction. Traditional expectations of the roles of doctor and patient are also changing with a corresponding impact on public and personal levels of the doctor–patient interaction. Within the public domain, to the extent that a patient is a customer, the agenda and parameters for a successful outcome should now be set much more on the patient's terms (S. Smith 1998). At a personal level, not all doctors are equally able or willing to surrender a more traditional paternalism in an effort to meet customer demand. They may experience particular difficulty with phases of the clinical transaction marked by the need for collaborative discussion. Indeed, studies have shown that these phases are in any case often omitted altogether, especially by those doctors with doctor-centred styles (Byrne and Long 1976). Not all patients, however, are capable or willing to assume the autonomy and control implicit in the change from the traditional patient role to the new role of customer.

The change in the balance of power within the clinical transaction that the new roles imply is likely, in any case, to be difficult to sustain throughout the transaction. As discussed in Chapter 4, there are sometimes powerful emotional forces at work in the clinical transaction, often enhanced by the effects of illness itself. These are usually underwritten by differences between patient and doctor in terms of knowledge, expertise, social status and the ownership and arrangement of the physical setting. All of this tips the balance of power in the doctor's favour especially, as we have seen, during physical examination. Nevertheless, to the extent that they do operate, such changes increase the potential for conflicts in role expectations and they correspondingly increase the potential for complication of the clinical transaction.

> **Mrs Porter**
> *Mrs Porter complained to her doctor of a pain in her ribs which had been present for some weeks. She attributed this pain to a muscle strained while gardening and asked her doctor to refer her for acupuncture. The doctor, knowing her to be a smoker, and noticing that she appeared to have lost some weight, felt that at least he should send Mrs Porter for a chest X-ray. Mrs Porter was very unhappy at this suggestion and, indeed, refused to go. She said that she thought treatments like acupuncture were available nowadays and was obviously disappointed when the doctor, in turn, refused to refer her. They parted with the problem of her pain undiagnosed and with no agreed plans to investigate further or treat it.*

In a complicated clinical transaction the doctor and the patient clearly had different expectations about their respective roles and attendant responsibilities. Mrs Porter felt that she understood the cause of her problem and did not, therefore, require the doctor's diagnosis. She also believed that she had a right to choose for herself the treatment she wanted. The doctor, on the other hand, was unhappy because he believed Mrs Porter's symptoms needed investigation in order to make a 'proper' medical diagnosis or at least to exclude serious disease. Neither of them appeared ready to negotiate an acceptable compromise. Mrs Porter certainly did not get what she had come for.

It is not at all clear that the rise of the patient as consumer has in fact shifted the balance of power very far in favour of the patient. That health promotion has been attributed such an important place in the agenda of the clinical transaction may have little to do directly with either the patient's or the doctor's own immediate concerns. After all, symptoms of health do not usually encourage the patient to visit a doctor. Well person clinics apart, issues of health promotion are often tacked on to the end of consultations, prompted by an agenda set externally by health politicians. How patients and doctors approach the task of health promotion therefore in part depends on how far they view this task as an unwelcome intrusion into the clinical transaction (see Chapter 7). Perhaps because of this, much health promotion in general practice proceeds under the auspices of the practice nurse and health visitor and in secondary care and community settings is often undertaken by non-medical health professionals.

Strategies employed to promote health can be seen to be both collective and individual. Individually, patients may seek help or advice from their doctors concerning their present and future health, which individual doctors are more or less willing and able to provide. The government, via its health policy, seeks to influence and promote the health of society at large. Some sociologists and doctors question the value of the health promotion enterprise as a whole, being uncertain of its efficacy or concerned that health promoting strategies run the risk of 'policing' health, rather than empowering and improving the lot of individuals (Beauchamp 1997). Be that as it may, strategies for health promotion can be usefully viewed as a fourfold typology depending on whether the methods used are authoritative or negotiated and the focus collective or individual (Figure 6.1) (Beattie 1991).

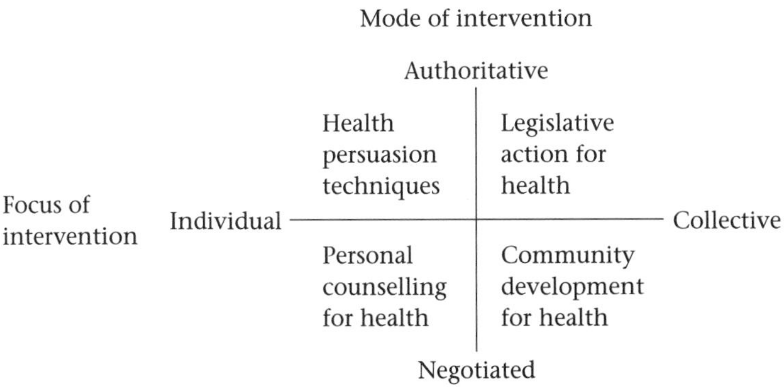

Mode of intervention

Authoritative

	Health persuasion techniques	Legislative action for health	
Focus of intervention — Individual			Collective
	Personal counselling for health	Community development for health	

Negotiated

Figure 6.1 Beattie's typology of health promotion (from Nettleton 1995: 242)

That different approaches and methods overlap is important for the doctor to bear in mind.

Health promotion as part of the clinical transaction

Face to face in the clinical transaction, doctor and patient are subject to all the external influences discussed above. Patients have ideas about health deriving from family, community, media and programmes of mass education. Doctors also have their own ideas, in part based on medical theory. But they too are subject to the influence of media and mass education. They may have considerably less expertise in health promotion than in the diagnosis and treatment of disease. Health promotion is an area of concern *par excellence* in which negotiated understandings become crucial if patient and doctor are to continue to go along together. Intrinsic counselling skills, in terms of monitoring the clinical transaction for any departures or complications and intervening where necessary, are consequently of paramount importance.

Considering Beattie's model (Figure 6.1), the doctor's strategy for health promotion within the clinical transaction is focused, most immediately and directly, on the individual. Risk factors for the individual patient need to be identified and agreed. Patients can then be educated about these and how their future health might be affected. Changes in behaviour, both in relation to identified risk and in terms of healthy living generally, need to be discussed. Whether or not this will provide sufficient motivation for the patient to change behaviour or alter a lifestyle and what impact this will have on the health of the population, are important but exceedingly difficult questions to answer (Nettleton 1995; Sidell *et al.* 1997).

It is the central premise of this book that, where possible, doctors should use their consulting skills to 'go together' with the patient (see Chapter 2); intrinsic counselling skills foster this collaborative endeavour and guide the clinical transaction along a straightforward path. Within the clinical transaction, therefore, the strategy of health promotion that should be adopted is one which, like Beattie's 'individual counselling for health' (Figure 6.1), is tailored to the individual patient. To be effective, health promotion within the clinical transaction should aim at empowering the patient to take the decisions and pursue the actions that are likely to improve and maintain health (Tones 1997). This requires that patient and doctor have and share relevant knowledge. The patient's knowledge and beliefs need first to be explored before the doctor seeks to educate the patient appropriately.

Health education, whether collective or individual, is an integral part of health promotion. The Society of Public Health Educators of America frame this endeavour within the following ethic:

> Health educators value privacy, dignity and the worth of the individual, and use skills consistent with these values. Health educators observe the principle of informed consent with respect to individuals and groups served. Health educators support change by choice, not by coercion.
>
> (quoted in Tones 1997: 36)

Impediments to change

Health education alone, however, may not be enough to change behaviour (Beauchamp 1997). If they are to be effective as health promoters, doctors must also make themselves aware of the impediments that exist which might prevent patients from putting knowledge into action. Such impediments are both personal and structural. The latter depend on social, geographical and economic factors that most individuals can do little to alter. Those factors which are personal and psychological may depend on attributes of personality and ways of relating which are also difficult to change. In many cases impediments to change combine personal and structural elements. When it comes to giving up smoking, for example, there may be considerable pressure from a peer group to continue (as well as the effect of tobacco advertising). Doctors need to take account of these obstacles to change as they apply to each of their patients, if they are to facilitate patients' efforts to make required and agreed modifications of lifestyle.

Of particular interest to us in this book are those impediments which might arise as a result of the interaction of doctor and patient within the clinical transaction. If taken by both to be a legitimate part of the transaction, i.e. a shared expectation within the public domain, health promotion should be a phase marked, more than any other, by the participation of patient and doctor as equals. When proceeding straightforwardly, the public–personal equilibrium of the clinical transaction during this phase is likely to be comfortably within the functional range for both doctor and patient. Relating as equals, however, may be difficult for either or both parties if it necessitates a change from habitual styles of consulting or ways of relating generally. The effort that such a change imposes may be enough to strain the public–personal equilibrium of patient or doctor. This may result in losing patience with the 'health promotion' work of the clinical transaction or ostensibly continuing with it at the public level but without any personal level engagement.

Other aspects of health promotion may also threaten the public–personal equilibrium of the clinical transaction. As we have implied, having to deal with issues of health promotion can be felt by the doctor or the patient as an unwarranted intrusion into the clinical transaction. If so, whether or not it is acknowledged, this may cause doctors to avoid or downgrade attention to important and legitimate areas of concern. If broached by the patient, matters of health promotion may then be dealt with only briefly or inadequately by the doctor. Furthermore, the negative emotion felt by the doctor is likely to communicate itself to the patient impairing the quality of the interaction between them.

Aspects of health promotion can raise anxiety-provoking possibilities of ill-health and the dangers that lead to premature death (as in the case of Mr Lewis, see pp. 66–7). Doctors and patients may therefore avoid bringing these issues onto the agenda, or collude in ignoring them. In these circumstances the anxiety that results can unbalance the public–personal equilibrium to the extent that it prevents the doctor or the patient fully engaging on both levels with the issues raised. Doctors and patients may be affected differently in these circumstances. They may well have different responses to different risks, for example, the risk of heart disease or cancer, because of personal or collectively held beliefs about such diseases. Cancer is often more feared than heart disease, for instance, and in some cases felt to be personally stigmatizing (Sontag 1977). This may mean that while some issues are dealt with, others are ignored. Sexual health may be another area that is particularly difficult to discuss especially if there are gender or age differences between patient and doctor.

The contemporary emphasis on lifestyles as important determinants of health tends to place responsibility for health onto the individual. Patients, therefore, often feel guilty about unhealthy behaviour such as smoking. As with fear of fatal disease, feelings such as guilt are also difficult to discuss meaningfully, without straining the public–personal equilibrium. Through interactive effects, health promotion can take on a moralistic tone, with doctors taking the part of judge or confessor and patients the part of perpetrator or sinner, bearing a personal guilt for their own ill-health. Such a dynamic will almost certainly push the public–personal equilibrium beyond its functional range so that personal level aspects come to dominate the transaction.

Doctors are helped to prevent such a situation developing if they remember that there are always structural factors influencing any aspect of behaviour. Changing behaviour is rarely a simple matter of choosing freely to do so. Doctors need, therefore, to share their understanding of the causes of ill-health in all its complexity and acknowledge impediments to change, if they are to empower patients to change those aspects which fall within their capacity so to do.

The influences which are brought to bear on the clinical transaction often derive from other groups or systems to which patients and doctors belong (see Chapter 7). This is particularly true of matters relating to health promotion. For example, when discussing contraception or the risk of sexually transmitted diseases, the religious beliefs of the patient or the doctor may be influential. There are many aspects of health about which doctors and patients inevitably hold personal beliefs or points of view which derive from the medical and non-medical systems of which they are members. When a doctor's beliefs are not pertinent to clinical concerns, care should be taken to ensure that they do not intrude into the clinical transaction. Sometimes, however, differences in beliefs may have to be dealt with as part of the work of the public domain, if they are not to complicate the clinical transaction. Certain doctors, for example, feel this to be necessary if asked to arrange or perform termination of pregnancy.

Attitudes, however, may not be sufficiently thought out to be expressible as beliefs or opinions. When they derive from professional, family or social groups, attitudes about health may be entirely outside a person's immediate awareness. This is particularly true of attitudes concerning the responsibility for illness and where it should lie. Such attitudes often become manifest only as complications within the clinical transaction, for example when patients fail to comply with treatment or advice or their feathers are ruffled in one way or another. Such complications, of course, may derive as much from the doctor's attitudes as those of the patient. This demands self-awareness on the part of the doctor and the intrinsic counselling skill to be able to monitor the clinical transaction for any signs that differences in attitude are causing departures which might complicate the transaction. Resolving such differences as part of the public level work may be necessary but the effort is time-consuming and often unsuccessful. Because of this, doctors may be tempted to ignore altogether legitimate areas of concern about a patient's health.

Miss Wallace

At 76, Miss Wallace was becoming increasingly disabled by osteoarthritis. More and more she tended to spend long periods sitting in her chair watching television. She found it hard to get about and to manage her shopping. She quite frequently called her GP to visit her and asked for pain-relieving medication. Miss Wallace said she should be in a 'home' and properly looked after but although financially secure she resented the financial implications, having paid income tax throughout her long working life. The doctor thought that her arthritis was, in fact, not too severe. She was free of other serious diseases and, in the interests of her general health, he felt she should be more physically active. He found her constant complaints a little wearing and so referred her to a domiciliary physiotherapist, whom he knew took a particularly robust view towards getting patients back on their feet and living independently. Miss Wallace refused to see the physiotherapist after her first visit; little changed except that relations with her doctor became even more strained. Eventually she did move into an elderly persons' home and the calls to the doctor became much less frequent.

Miss Wallace and her doctor had very different ideas about what was optimal for her present and future well-being. Miss Wallace felt that she deserved to be looked after by the 'state' having contributed financially for so much of her life. She did not believe or appreciate her doctor's contention that her health would be better if she were more active and might suffer if she were 'looked after'. Her doctor believed strongly that everyone should retain independence and live in their own homes for as long as possible. He tired of Miss Wallace's complaining attitude and partly to escape the frequent visits he referred her to the domiciliary physiotherapist. The result was that Miss Wallace became offended and even more entrenched in her position, providing little opportunity for the physiotherapist to deploy any of the therapeutic and negotiating skills she might possess.

Conclusions

Health is not simply the absence of disease. It is hard to define and health beliefs and attitudes have diverse origins. Doctors are not the experts on health in quite the same way as they are on the clinical management of disease. Health has become big business and many vested interests seek to infuence how health is defined as well as to influence opinion as to the best methods for promoting it. Partly for these reasons there has been a movement away from medical paternalism towards health consumerism. Nonetheless, in the UK, for political and economic reasons, health promotion has gained increasing importance in the government's health agenda, both in terms of public health measures and as part of the clinical transaction. Taken together, these factors have profound implications for doctors and patients engaging in clinical transactions.

More than with any other goal of the clinical transaction, the success of health promotion depends on the collaborative engagement of doctor and patient as equals. For many doctors and patients this is likely to necessitate a change in the usual ways they relate to each other. Such changes can strain the appropriate public–personal equilibrium within the clinical transaction sufficiently to cause departures from the straightforward. The situation may be further aggravated by negative feelings about having to tackle issues to do with health promotion. Among other things, health promotion may be resented as the intrusion of an externally set agenda or felt to be an invasion of the patient's privacy. It may also evoke anxiety about disease or premature death. The overall effect of such factors is to make it more difficult, and sometimes impossible, for either or both parties to engage appropriately with health promotion activity at both public and personal levels.

Health promotion is usually directed at changing some aspect of a patient's lifestyle. The patient's role in these circumstances is different from that of the sick role which is usually adopted with the support of those around. On the contrary, altering aspects of lifestyle may mean ostracism from peer or social groups because the patient no longer participates in mutually defining behaviour but instead draws attention to its unhealthiness. Impediments to change not only are to be located within patients but also may depend on factors in their social, economic or geographical environment which are beyond their direct control. Unless doctors take full account of this there is a risk not only that they will expect patients to take full responsibility for their own health but also that patients will take the blame, and feel the guilt, for their own ill-health. The result may be a moralistic attitude towards health which runs counter to an ethic of empowering individuals to take what ever control they can of the factors which promote health or pose a risk to it.

As with all aspects of the clinical transaction, when dealing with matters of health promotion, the clinical transaction must be monitored for any departures from the straightforward. This entails doctors being aware of and sensitive to their own attitudes and assumptions, as well as fears or difficulties in broaching issues which might cause anxiety, shame or affront. The influence of systems outside the clinical transaction are particularly important, especially if they are not supportive of changes demanded in lifestyle. Making patients aware of self-help groups, or directly involving family or friends can be productive.

Harmonious communication between the different levels of the hierarchy of health care resulting in consistent messages about health promoting activity helps individual doctors to help individual patients. It may thereby also help secure those global objectives of health for all set by the 1986 WHO conference in

Ottawa. Although it remains uncertain what it is that best promotes health, in the absence of harmonization, within and without the clinical transaction, the best efforts of health professionals are unlikely to succeed.

Chapter 7

Clinical teams and systems of health care

> A system in this case consists of the internal world of the individual, comprising his [*sic*] beliefs and expectations together with his primitive inborn impulses and the controls that he has developed over them. Nevertheless, he exists as an open system and must interact with the world in which he lives, continually striving to maintain a balance between his own internal needs and the demands of others.
>
> (Robert de Board 1978: 89)

Introduction

Many professional structures, such as the General Medical Council (GMC), the Royal Colleges and NHS 'management', exert an influence on medical practice. Some of this influence is perceived by doctors as reflecting concern about fiscal policy rather than medical care or health promotion. As such it can be experienced as an intrusion into the clinical transaction with a particular patient. Within the hierarchy of health care as a whole, the clinical transaction between patient and doctor is often the final common pathway for the provision of health care but it can also bear the brunt of any such intrusion. Maintaining an appropriate balance between the clinical transaction's 'internal needs' and the 'demands of others' can therefore impose a significant additional burden on doctors.

Understanding the influence of the 'supra-systems', higher in the organizational hierarchy and with wider objectives for the health service and standards of medical care, is clearly important for doctors and for other professionals involved. Managers argue for the doctor's awareness of the financial cost of treating or not treating a given patient or condition. Many other non-medical groupings, for example medical sociologists, community health councils or patients' participation groups, also wish doctors to take into account and value a range of factors which are external to the actual clinical transaction.

A very ill patient requiring expensive treatment may understandably wish to have a doctor who does not think about how the taxpayer's money could be better spent elsewhere. We take the view, however, that it is no longer possible or desirable for doctors to practise their art and science as if isolated on a desert island but with limitless financial and other resources. Nonetheless, there is a balance to be struck, if not at each clinical transaction then with many of them, which takes into account and reflects aspects of the wider systems in which the clinical transaction itself is embedded. If a suitable balance is not achieved then the result may be a disturbance of the public–personal equilibrium of the clinical transaction between individual patient and doctor. This in turn may lead to departures from the straightforward and the development of a complicated clinical transaction. As an aspect of their intrinsic counselling skills, therefore, doctors need to appraise both the nature and quality of the relationship between the system of the clinical transaction and the systems with which it interacts.

Doctors' systems

Practising doctors are not free agents. They need to be licensed on a renewable basis, subject to their maintaining basic standards of medical care and professionalism. They are also required to be insured, to guarantee financial security in the event of litigation involving their professional activities. Like other workers, they are contracted to work in a particular setting with colleagues, for some of whom they may be directly responsible and for others they themselves will be responsible. In this way, each doctor is a member of a number of systems, which may overlap with or be related hierarchically to others (Figure 7.1).

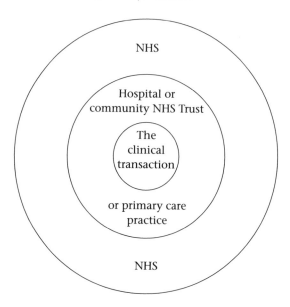

Figure 7.1 Hierarchical systems of health care

Hierarchical systems

Ideally, the influence of all the supra-systems hierarchically related to the clinical transaction is a supportive one, their goals readily harmonizing. Systems higher in the hierarchy aim to both define and encourage the achievement of relevant medical tasks and set acceptable standards of care. In this way, doctors are enabled to understand clearly what it is they are expected to carry out within a given setting (and for which they are remunerated). In practice, however, the different levels in the hierarchy of systems, all of which ultimately impinge on the doctor, may not harmonize in terms of their aims and how these aims translate into the work of the individual clinical transaction.

> ### Mr Green
> *Mr Green was a consultant surgeon, with a small private practice, who chose to put the bulk of his professional energy into his NHS work. He frequently worked longer than his contracted hours. However, his employing NHS Trust*

introduced new parking arrangements, in order to raise money. The Trust's financial objective meant that Mr Green's tightly managed schedule, allowing him his own private practice, was embarrassed. (The Trust's objective was not in harmony with his own financial objective.) He now had to undertake an additional five minutes' walk from his car to the operating theatre. For two mornings every week this meant that he was marginally late for his operating list. This upset Mr Green since he had always prided himself on his punctuality, expecting no less from those working with him. For a time, he was uncharacteristically irritable and at times hostile to members of his team whom he believed would think the worse of him for his lateness.

Overlapping systems

As well as being members of systems which relate hierarchically, doctors are inevitably members of other systems which overlap (Figure 7.2). The clinical transaction, for example, is a system of which doctor and patient are members. They are also members of separate family systems which, therefore, overlap with that of the clinical transaction. By virtue of this automatic member-ship of other overlapping systems, doctors are also subject to their influence. These systems may not be part of the health care

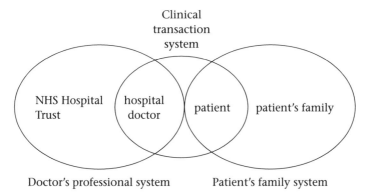

Figure 7.2 Overlapping systems

system and are not therefore 'medical'. They nonetheless exert an effect which, in some circumstances, can adversely change the doctor's attitudes and behaviour and thereby affect how treatment is delivered, if not actual medical practice.

> **Mr Jones**
> *Mr Jones had very reluctantly accepted a psychiatric referral on account of his sexual dysfunction. He felt his symptom to be shaming, not least because in his culture sexual potency was particularly highly valued. His embarrassing predicament had been helped by his confiding in his female GP. After months of support and quiet coaxing from her, he had been persuaded to seek skilled psychological help. He was dismayed, therefore, to find himself face-to-face with a male psychiatrist from his own culture, who was also of a similar age. Mr Jones's manner was aggressive and he told the psychiatrist that he had kept the outpatient appointment only to placate his GP and that the problem was not particularly troublesome and had now virtually disappeared in any case. Clearly agitated and visibly sweating, he left the consulting room.*

Cultural dimensions, while important, need not be disadvantageous to the pursuit of the goals of a clinical transaction, even though it turned out to be so in the above example. It may be more often the case that similarity is helpful. The main point to be made is that doctors and patients cannot choose to be culturally other than they are. Nor can they simply dismiss the legacy of associated cultural beliefs, which proved to be both powerful and unhelpful in the case of Mr Jones.

As in matters of culture and ethnic origin, similarities or differences between doctors and patients may be obvious and a matter of fact rather than opinion. Other differences or similarities, however, though relatively indiscernible, may still be highly influential, albeit subtly so, in their effect on a given clinical transaction. As professionals, doctors are likely to betray aspects of themselves that locate them within a particular class or social structure. In addition, age, gender, physical attractiveness, to say nothing of some idiosyncratic aspects of personality, are outside the doctor's direct and conscious control. Though not a matter of choice, these factors still exert an effect within the clinical transaction, partly through the associated beliefs and attitudes which are perceived by the patient to accompany them. Age, for example, was an important factor in the example of Mr Jones and also with Danny (see pp. 96, 24). In Danny's case, of course, it was not only that the new diabetologist was younger but that this doctor had a very different consultation style, partly deriving from a different set of personality attributes from those of the original paediatric consultant. The situation was compounded by the fact that Danny's family circumstances were such that he was more comfortable with a *grand*father-figure than a father-figure.

The various systems of family and friends also influence the doctor in ways, and to degrees, which can impinge on the clinical transaction. Just 'getting out of the wrong side of the bed' can mean that the first outpatient consultation or the first surgical incision is adversely affected by the doctor's mood. An argument at home, perhaps, can result in the doctor's next human contact with a potentially friendly receptionist being imbued with less than the usual bonhomie. In this way, others may receive an emotional volley or burden which does not rightly belong to them.

In these instances, trying to identify what belongs where and to whom is not easy. But it does repay time and thought to consider the matter, since sometimes the interaction between the system of the clinical transaction and its surrounding systems can unhelpfully amplify any initial difficulty.

Danny

The new consultant's outpatient clinic on a Monday morning was always particularly busy and, being new in his post, he had not felt able to change it either by offering fewer appointments or trying to obtain better medical and nursing support. He found himself sleeping poorly on Sunday night and in order to relieve this began taking a little alcohol to which he was unaccustomed. This left him feeling worse still on a Monday morning and only more adversely affected by the excessive workload of the clinic which he felt increasingly powerless to influence. This had been the emotional, personal-level backdrop to his first meeting with Danny.

Patients' systems

The effect of the patient's membership of different systems is no less influential in its potential effect on the clinical transaction than that of the doctor's and in many instances is very similar to it. Patients belong to certain systems by virtue of their age, gender, ethnic origin, occupation, social class and culture. They thereby also acquire any rights and responsibilities, freedom and constraints, which accompany membership of a system. As with doctors, family members and friends of patients, who are influential elements of the systems to which patients belong, can directly or indirectly support or undermine the clinical transaction. Mrs Bradley's hectic work schedule and home life had meant that the only respite in the week was her Friday evening session with her sympathetic GP (see pp. 24–35). In this case the family resented that they had to fend for themselves on a Friday and ridiculed her regular attendance. Mrs Bradley's guilt about letting down her family meant that her compliance with the treatment for her irritable bowel was poor.

Types of intervention

Taking a systems perspective can allow the doctor to consider how contextual influences can complicate a clinical transaction, as in the example of Mrs Bradley and her family. Once these influences are recognized, doctors need to decide how best they might deal with the external situation. A range of approaches is available.

First, the doctor may discuss openly with the patient how external elements, imported into the clinical transaction, are exerting a complicating effect. This means bringing onto the public level of the transaction aspects of the patient's outside life which they may not have realized were hampering progress towards desired clinical goals. Second, the complicating element itself, for example, a patient's problematic relationship with a partner, may be directly involved in the clinical transaction through inviting the other party to become part of it. This might simply be a one-off, information-gathering exercise or become a more prolonged matter, as in couples counselling or family therapy. Third, the complicating element, for example the parents of a child, may be enlisted to help (rather than hinder) the delivery of some aspect of treatment or health care. Parents or other carers may be physically available to the patient at times and in ways that the professionals are not. Fourth, when a complicating element is another professional or other agency, respective roles and responsibilities may need to be clarified in order to avoid inconsistency or unnecessary and unhelpful duplication of tasks. This may be done by convening meetings of those involved, as in a case conference.

> ### Ms Carter
>
> *Ms Carter had longstanding urinary problems from childhood and had received surgical intervention on a number of occasions, although this had brought little symptomatic relief. The surgery had also resulted in the formation of a fistula and given rise to bowel adhesions which were also occasionally troublesome. Not surprisingly, there were psychological sequelae since the fistula had drastically impaired Ms Carter's longstanding low self-esteem and she had become phobic of sexual contact and other intimacy. She had regular outpatient clinic visits to a variety of hospital departments.*
>
> *Ms Carter's GP was increasingly concerned that each hospital department worked as if in isolation. While the 'physical medicine' staff tended to view her as 'stoical and cheery', the GP received reports from the psychiatrist that the patient was at times 'close to suicidal despair'. The frequent visits for her physical ailments, which were not curable, had the effect of raising unrealistic expectations and a false optimism. Each visit was followed by a transient return of serious depressive feelings. The GP decided therefore to convene a meeting of himself and the three consultants involved to obtain a more realistic and holistic view. After this had been established Ms Carter was invited to join a further meeting of all concerned to discuss matters, with beneficial effect.*

The overall aim of the interventions outlined in Ms Carter's case was to attempt to harmonize the goals of the relevant overlapping systems of the various hospital departments. If such an aim is to be achieved, doctors must remain sensitive and alert to incompatible goals which undermine the work of the clinical transaction. This means that doctors should cultivate their aware-ness and understanding of such influences, both as they affect themselves and their patients (see Chapter 8). This enables them to monitor the clinical transaction for these effects – an import-ant aspect of intrinsic counselling skills. Although some impedi-ments have to be accepted as givens and as immovable, many can be altered or ameliorated in their effect, even if not completely removed. Constructing transaction windows (see pp. 26–30) for each overlapping system in which doctor and patient are involved can help show how and where one system might be effecting another (see Norton and Smith 1994: 67–83).

Clinical multidisciplinary teams

Much medical work is carried out in clinical teams. Some may be so dispersed or diverse in their composition that it may not always be obvious that they are in fact teams. Nonetheless, in so far as they are, they can be construed as systems. A doctor, for example, is inherently part of the health care system (including laboratory services, blood transfusion staff, etc.), even when work-ing single-handedly in a remote, rural general practice setting. (Of course, it may not feel to the individual doctor like being part of a team or system and even knowing it intellectually may be but cold comfort.)

Where the clinical team is obvious or literally present in the same room, as in a practice meeting, a psychiatric ward round or a case conference about a child or elderly person, it may still not seem that everybody is in the team or is playing the same game and adhering to the same professional rules. There may be a marked diversity of views or a clear parting of the ways.

> #### Sub-teams
> *A consultant psychiatrist and social worker from the same community mental health team had each visited in his home a disturbed young man who was known to suffer from schizophrenia. The consultant, who was the first to make an assessment, considered that the patient required compulsory inpatient admission, (i.e. under a 'Section' of the Mental*

Health Act 1983). The social worker, visiting later that same morning, felt that increasing the frequency of visits by the team's community psychiatric nurse would suffice. The consultant and social worker, the senior members of the team, were at loggerheads during the afternoon's ward round with neither willing to give ground. The rest of the team eventually joined in the heated argument which developed, some taking one side and some the other.

The clinical team itself, as in the example, behaves as if it is made up of sub-teams (i.e. subsystems) each of which has its own slightly different set of views and aims. Such differences, of course, can be beneficial when they lead to fertile discussion or to a previously unconsidered solution to a given problem. Often, however, a team may find itself repeatedly encountering the same or similar stubborn stalemate from which only sterile outcomes are possible. Such situations sap morale and easily lead to staff sickness, absenteeism and other undesirable consequences (Miller 1989).

Where such stalemate exists, as with stalemate in a clinical transaction, the interaction within a team can be usefully analysed in terms of its public and personal level elements. This may reveal tensions which are not otherwise obvious, some of which can be resolved through a careful understanding of the public and personal level contributions of the team's separate members. It must be remembered that not all team members are equal and the formal hierarchical structure of the team may not be equally palatable or acceptable to all. Alongside the formal structure are likely to be one or more informal hierarchies, which may compete. These can function as 'anti-teams', scuppering the team's formal (public level) attempts to collaborate (Obholzer 1994).

Doctors are often the leaders of clinical teams and therefore have a major responsibility for trying to ensure, as far as possible, that the team functions effectively in its clinical, public level role. As we shall see, this can prove to be a complex and arduous task. Some doctors are suited to it by virtue of their personality, interactive style and value system. They enjoy the challenge that it represents. Others may dread it. In any event, leading a team depends on being able to keep the team's public level goals clearly in view, while also remaining sensitive to any signs of departure, at either public or interpersonal levels. In particular, it involves an appreciation of the interface between the team's overall functioning and the individual clinical transactions in which its members are involved.

Cracks and splits

When under stress, teams are likely to show 'cracks' or 'splits' reflecting potential or actual functional fragmentation into subsystems (Gabbard 1986). Evidence of these can be obvious, especially when revealed at the personal level in displays of temper or other emotional outbursts. They can also become manifest in public level aspects of the team's work, such as 'bad' clinical practice or 'poor' clinical judgement. It is, therefore, especially important under such circumstances for doctors to remain alert to signs of cracking or splitting. Adequate team functioning may decay into warring subsystems, often along 'fault lines' which could have been predicted. The nature and relationship of the subsystems may, for example, reflect different disciplines, older versus newer staff, whole-time versus part-time staff, day versus shift workers or night staff, better paid versus worse paid, and so on. Such obvious cracks relating to team function, however, do not always betray the origin of a problem which may lie in hidden and complex interpersonal conflict nor do they offer insights as to how best a doctor might intervene to resolve tensions.

> *Cracks*
> *A small inpatient psychotherapy unit was dependent on a hospital canteen in an adjacent large mental hospital which, however, was downsizing prior to its closure. Walking to lunch afforded all staff in the multidisciplinary team a chance to mingle and mix on an informal basis. Discussions over lunch were usually animated and seldom involved 'work' topics. Following the closure of the canteen, those staff who had their own offices tended to bring packed lunches and eat them in solitude. Those who did not have an office had to make their way to the new canteen, which was a short car journey away. Only some of those staff members had their*

own transport. Some previously amicable public level, collaborative aspects of work began to take on a more negative interpersonal tone.

On superficial examination, in the example, it had seemed to the consultant leading the team that the loss of the canteen facility would have an equal impact on everybody. After all, the whole team had previously used it. In fact, the closure of the canteen meant the breakdown of important, albeit informal, communication within the team and it also had a vastly different effect on individual team members. The interactive effect of departures at the personal level (i.e. the different emotional responses to the changes within the team) was to impair the professional, working relationships at the public level in subtle ways. In fact, although an initial acrimonious debate about the canteen closure subsided, the disagreement between individual staff members continued and started to affect apparently unconnected public level issues to do with patients and their care. The consultant was eventually able, through the use of multiple transaction windows (see Chapter 2), to disentangle his own personal reaction to the closure of the canteen from those of his colleagues.

It can be difficult, if not impossible, to say precisely where or when a given departure, complication or shift in the public–personal equilibrium of a team started. In practice, it may be sufficient to monitor the current state of affairs, rather than discover its original cause, but consider steps to rectify it. Multidisciplinary and other clinical teams function as ongoing, dynamic groupings in which, in a sense, the team can be construed as having its own public–personal equilibrium which can be upset. As in the case of the clinical transaction, this equilibrium can be shifted so that personal or public level aspects dominate unproductively (see Chapter 4). At a given point in time, therefore, the team functions with greater or lesser success in achieving its public level goals. Interpersonal factors, as with the clinical transaction, can promote or impede the public level function.

In the aftermath of an episode such as that concerning the canteen closure and its effect on team function, the team may be particularly susceptible to any influences which exploit the 'cracks' set up or revealed. Sometimes these influences are external to the team. In other instances, however, they will reflect aspects of the clinical work of the team which are directly and intimately bound up with the care of individual patients. Where more than one member is involved in the treatment of a single patient, particularly in the context of long-term illness in an inpatient setting, staff may become polarized in terms of their assessment and evaluation of a patient's problem and the treatment required. Existing 'cracks', such as between shiftworkers and '9 to 5' staff, can then be deepened to become 'splits'. Aspects of the clinical work at the level of the various clinical transactions between the individual team members and the particular patient become amplified and can polarize other, if not all, members of the team (Main 1957).

Splits

A 30-year-old man with longstanding forensic and psychiatric problems was attending a psychiatric day hospital. He frustrated the staff's attempts to rehabilitate him because, at the point of discharge, he would become acutely suicidal and all plans to reintegrate him back into the wider community would be shelved. He had himself been severely sexually and physically abused and perhaps because of this most staff in the multidisciplinary team saw him as a victim who had made considerable strides in establishing some self-esteem and self-confidence. For the most part he was kindly and helpful, especially to other physically frail and immobile patients. At other times, however, he would appear to be callous and on one occasion he held a member of staff hostage for thirty minutes before releasing the person unharmed. He was subsequently very penitent.

After yet another shelving of discharge plans, the team members became quite polarized. Some, who experienced themselves as sympathetic and kindly, considered that the setting of a discharge date imposed too great a pressure on the patient. They disparaged the views of others who felt that all their patience and tolerance was at an end and the patient should now be discharged whether or not appropriate aftercare was in place. The two sides could not agree, at least for a time, until it was realized within the team that the 'split' in the staff closely resembled the unintegrated inner world of the patient – solicitous or callous – with little in between.

The team leader

To manage the above 'split' team situation required the consultant not only to attend to the dynamic staff relationships but also to consider the patient around whom the splitting effect had developed. Distinguishing between cracks and splits is therefore important. 'Splits' develop as the result of staff involvement with a particular patient, even though the split may well exploit previously existing cracks. The emotional dynamics which characterize the splitting of the staff mirror the powerful dynamics operating for the patient. The development of 'cracks', by contrast, does not require the direct participation of the patient or sub-group of patients.

In deciding what action to take, especially as team leaders, doctors need to be able to distinguish between cracks and splits, a task which can be especially difficult if they themselves are caught up in the divisive process. As a detached onlooker, it is easier to discern both the presence of cracks and splits and also potentially to distinguish them. Although sometimes very prominent in the psychiatric contexts discussed earlier, similar mechanisms operate in other teams such as the primary health care team. In these situations team leaders may have little experience in their clinical training which prepares them for the task of unravelling the consequences of 'cracks' and 'splits'.

When caught up in these situations, however, there are some useful pointers which can alert doctors to the fact that splitting is going on (Gabbard 1986). Foremost is the extent to which there is a conviction of being absolutely right and having the whole 'truth'. The more stridently one holds a view the more likely one is to be involved in splitting. (Being 'caught up' implies that a doctor's usual public–personal equilibrium has shifted, usually so that the personal level dominates.) Another helpful marker is the difficulty in re-establishing the usual equilibrium, for example, how difficult it is to calm down after debating the situation in question. Other markers might be the taking home of more anxiety than usual relating to the workplace, having dreams or nightmares relating to the work situation, wishing to avoid certain clinical team meetings for fear of being embroiled in arguments, or, indeed, the opposite, i.e. relishing such interactions or scheming to outwit and demolish the opposition!

Ordinarily, a doctor's professional work does not evoke such a 'life and death' reaction or threaten the very sense of professional or personal survival.

Meetings

Team meetings serve a number of functions which are relevant to both personal and public level concerns. Apart from ordinary or routine team business, they can re-establish interpersonal bonds and mitigate the relative isolation of much clinical work. In order to pay sufficiently close attention to the potential problems discussed above, the clinical team may need to put aside time to meet to evaluate their overall team function. Such an internal 'audit' of the team may reveal incipient or embryonic cracks or splits, some of which can be healed merely by an open airing of the relevant issues and so prevent deep cracks, and ultimately splits, from developing. Entrenched complicated clinical transactions are likely to require further meetings of the team, whose sole agenda is to focus on, understand more fully and resolve such issues. Such meetings may need to involve the whole team, or in some instances, only relevant subsystems of the team. It can be beneficial to engage the help of an appropriately skilled outside facilitator who can provide a more objective commentary on what is happening within the team.

Where the level of stress on staff is high and results from stressful or high levels of direct patient contact there should be frequent meetings as a matter of routine. They allow for the work of individual members of the team to be supervised, thus providing both learning opportunities and support as well as clinical guidance. This helps to safeguard good clinical practice and is of distinct benefit to patients. It also represents one aspect of preventative medicine in relation to the mental health of staff through the provision of appropriate supervision and support in the workplace.

Conclusions

Doctors inevitably work as members of teams or larger and broader systems of health care. They are also members of non-medical systems which nonetheless affect the ways they behave in their medical setting. The clinical transaction itself can be affected by influences arising in these external systems, with the result that its main goals remain unachieved or relegated in importance. Understanding the origins and effects of such influences, and how to correct them, involves the use of the doctor's intrinsic counselling skills. These can be enhanced where necessary by constructing transaction windows which can be adapted for use with teams, that is systems larger than the two-person system of the clinical transaction. Viewing the clinical transaction and the interacting systems, through transaction and 'systems' windows respectively, reveals important aspects of the effects of the relationships between systems.

Both overlapping and hierarchical relationships between systems need to be taken into account. The first sign of departure or complication may be detected within the clinical transaction itself or else within the wider, relating systems such as the clinical team. Complications at either level can feed up or down the hierarchy of systems and so affect the functioning of the team or the clinical transaction respectively. Similarly the functioning of teams may be affected by management decisions still higher up the hierarchy. If teams are dysfunctional, the goals set at this higher level may be jeopardized. Complications developing within a clinical transaction may be easily discernible. Because of its greater complexity, however, the dysfunctional team and its potential effect upon individual clinical transactions can be particularly difficult to assess. The more the doctor becomes personally involved, the harder it is to be objective.

Team members higher up in the formal hierarchy within the clinical team, and particularly the team leader, need to remain vigilant to the overall quality of team functioning. This means monitoring the degree to which the team as a whole is achieving its public level goals and also seeking to ensure that interpersonal relationships support this work. 'Cracks' and 'splits' develop in teams for many reasons. Splitting depends on the influence of an individual patient(s) on the functioning of a team, and not just on influences internal to the team system itself. In such cases it can be as if the psychopathology or style of interpersonal relating of individual patients, through interactive effects, exploits existing divisions in the team resulting in deep divisions or 'splits'. Where there is evidence that the team is dysfunctional, whether in terms of impaired interpersonal relationships or public role function (whether reflecting cracks or splits in a team), this needs to be detected and understood. Meetings of the whole team, and sometimes of its sub-teams, are essential if all the interrelating systems are to synergize their efforts and work together harmoniously for the patient's benefit.

Chapter 8

Implications for training

Learning depends on the individual's experiences within, for example, his or her family, social environment and, more specifically, the educational institutions he or she attends. Teaching involves the provision of those conditions that directly promote effective learning.

(L.B. Curzon 1990: 22)

Introduction

What is central to an application of the clinical transaction model is a capacity to distinguish between the doctor's public role (and its associated tasks and goals) and the personal reaction of the doctor to the patient, which is based on unique personality attributes. Training for such an undertaking begins long before specialized medical training is embarked upon, since without exception, future doctors at some time have themselves been patients in their own right. From such experiences they have learned something about the public role of the doctor having been on the receiving end of it. This also provides some insight into the rights and responsibilities of patients in performing their 'sick role'. Furthermore, the experience of daily living in society, with its cultural diversity and range of associated attitudes and beliefs towards medicine, has subliminally imbued future doctors with certain expectations of the roles of doctors and patients. They are, of course, also influenced by the media, which are important for conveying issues relating to the rights and responsibilities of both doctors and patients.

On entry to formal medical training, the future doctor is not therefore a naive student – a *tabula rasa* to be inscribed by his or her trainers. Rather, medical students are more or less formed personalities, with some idiosyncratic beliefs about illness and cure and also with particular personal aspects, including those which motivated their selection of medicine as a career. The net result is that some of the later public role responsibilities implicit in the doctor's social role will 'fit' a given doctor, without imposing an undue strain or requiring undue effort, but others will not. In so far as the patient, as consumer of the doctor's health care, is a grateful and satisfied customer, the doctor's self-esteem may even be enhanced by fulfilling the public level role. If so, the doctor is likely to remain unconcerned by, and uninterested in, the special requirements of the public level interaction with the patient. If such a satisfactory outcome does not result, however, not only may the doctor's public role performance be impaired but also there may be a negative impact on the personal level. The doctor may be puzzled, pained and personally deflated by the failure to achieve clinical transaction goals.

It can help, therefore, to learn in some detail what it is that doctors and patients must do to optimize the outcomes of their clinical transactions. Some aspects are already part of the curriculum: learning of clinical skills, consulting skills, interviewing skills, etc. How public and personal levels interact, however, is not routinely taught nor are those intrinsic counselling skills which are required to monitor the public–personal equilibrium pertaining to a given clinical transaction. In addition, even though much of the doctor's work is carried out as a member of a clinical team, the relevant skills with which to monitor the overall functioning of teams are not formally taught.

Pre-clinical training

The undergraduate curriculum for pre-clinical medical training already covers some relevant areas of the particular aspects of sociology and psychology which relate to the model of the clinical transaction as described in this book. Such academic aspects, however, may not be readily understood in terms of their integration into later clinical practice. The model presented here is thus relevant to pre-clinical studies since it embodies not only concepts of social role (including medical role) but sick role, abnormal illness behaviour and the psychoanalytic concepts of

transference-countertransference and the conscious and unconscious mind (see Chapter 3 and also Norton and Smith 1994).

Clinical training

At the clinical stage of medical training, the theoretical aspects
learnt at the pre-clinical stage start to be put into practice.
Through the face to face contact with patients, students experience at first hand the effects of interaction at public and personal
levels, as they begin to assume their professional roles. They also
encounter and interact with a variety of colleagues, some of whom
form part of a peer group, others of whom are part of the formal
teaching hierarchy. At this stage, the process of training means
necessarily a progression through clinical and other settings, both
formal and informal, involving patients, friends, colleagues and
teachers. Some of these different relationships demand the appropriate performance of a variety of public level roles – student,
doctor or representative, perhaps. Clinical medical students and
their teachers may not necessarily be aware of the rich and complex learning environment in which they are situated. Yet it can
be seen to be so when viewed from the combined perspective of
public and personal level interaction and the wider social context of medical training.

The richness of this total learning situation is not exploited
and is therefore never fully realized. In theory, however, training in the clinical transaction model utilizes certain of these
unexploited educational opportunities. Some of the informal aspects of the training process thereby become part of a discussion
which takes place in the formal teaching sessions. The student's
peer group itself can be used as a tool for experiential learning
about the difference between public and personal level interactions. For example, group meetings of students, set up and facilitated by trainers, can discuss the differences between meeting
informally (no public level agenda) and meeting formally (with
a public level agenda). With time, the agenda can be encouraged
to 'deepen', as the group gets more comfortable with itself. The
discussion can then begin to embrace more personal aspects,
including those resulting from dealings with patients, as well as
peers, senior colleagues and trainers. Some postgraduate courses

for general practice already incorporate this form of non-directive teaching (McEvoy 1993).

Discussing what it feels like to experience the demands of a public as opposed to a solely personal level interaction is likely to help clinical students to develop an ability to distinguish later between these two levels in the actual clinical setting. Becoming aware of how the personal level can change, in idiosyncratic or extreme ways which bear little or no relationship to the public level tasks, can be instructive. It highlights the complexity of the two-person clinical situation and the power of the personal level to distract one or both parties from the professional task and in other ways to undermine the professional endeavour. Importantly, utilizing the multi-person environment of training can facilitate an understanding of the influence of 'external' systems, including that of the peer group.

Also to be learned from such an experiential approach are techniques for elevating any relevant identified aspects of interactions at the personal level for open discussion at the public level. This skill is crucial to acquire since, within the clinical setting, such aspects may represent departures from a straightforward clinical transaction. The sooner training in these skills starts the better. Supervised clinical transactions between students and real (or simulated) patients can facilitate the development of such skills in actual clinical settings. The acquisition of relevant skills in most medical school curricula is most likely during psychiatric student placements, which also incorporate skills relating to the examination of a patient's mental state (Norton and Smith 1994). However, intrinsic counselling skills, although not routinely discussed or taught, are relevant to the whole of the clinical stage of medical training. They should not be learned only in relation to a patient's discrete psychopathology nor solely in the context of psychiatric diagnosis and treatment.

Pre-registration training

If fully conversant with and practised in the clinical transaction model, the trainee is better equipped to make sense of the significant shift from student status to being a doctor. This progression entails changes to both social role responsibilities and personal level aspects. Knowing about each of these, and having experienced and discussed their potential for unhelpful interaction, can help to soften what is sometimes the sharp psychological blow of qualification and the beginning of medical practice proper.

There is often little space and time for formal support and supervision during the pre-registration period but the informal support of peers and senior medical and non-medical colleagues is invaluable. The quality of such support can be enhanced if other professionals involved are also conversant with aspects of the clinical transaction previously described. This stage of the doctor's career often provides the first strong sense of belonging to a clinical team. Even though earlier attachments have also been team-based, it is likely that the pre-registration team attachments are both longer and stronger than earlier ones.

Being relatively junior in the hierarchy of the clinical team provides the pre-registration doctor with the opportunity to observe both public and personal level interactions and the difficulties encountered by the team in achieving its relevant goals. Some of the obstacles to achieving goals are seen to arise for obvious reasons but others apparently incomprehensibly. Some derive from personal level aspects and others from impediments at the public level.

Mr Evans

The specialist registrar was noted by the pre-registration house surgeon to be a kindly colleague who regularly took on, apparently enthusiastically, an amount of informal teaching during the operating lists. His demeanour changed, however, whenever the consultant was present. He then tended to ignore the rest of the surgical team and would become totally absorbed by the task of engaging the consultant in conversation. The registrar's asocial monopolization of the consultant and the exclusion of his other colleagues was so complete that the rest of the team sometimes felt embarrassed for him on account of his apparent disregard of ordinary social skills. The consultant, however, seemed to be quite oblivious to this.

The pre-registration doctor did not understand what lay behind the apparent personality change in Mr Evans.

Eventually, shortly before he himself was to move to his next post, he asked the registrar about what he had observed. It turned out that the consultant had promised to teach him a particular highly specialized surgical technique, the acquisition of which would equip him to apply for a range of prestigious consultant posts. The consultant, however, never seemed to have time for this. Although frustrated, the registrar felt unable to express this or to confront the consultant about the matter directly. It seemed to the house surgeon, therefore, that his senior colleague's somewhat sycophantic behaviour represented an indirect attempt at communicating a specific message. The attempt was perhaps doomed to failure since such a discreet message could not easily be divined by the consultant surgeon.

Ms Ingram

Another pre-registration doctor had repeatedly noted heated exchanges between the Old Age consultant and Ms Ingram, the Old Age Team's senior social worker. The issue tended to start, early in the ward round, with polite disagreement about decisions to discharge a particular elderly patient and the two proponents' differing assessments of the extent of the patient's needs and the adequacy and availability of support services outside the hospital with which to meet these. By the end of the ward round, the consultant and Ms Ingram would usually be disagreeing about almost everything, including the time of day. Most of the rest of the team seemed bemused by this chronic state of affairs but prepared for it to continue, without remark.

The house physician gleaned that, until the arrival of the particular social worker, the consultant had been particularly active in discharging his patients and aggressive in attitude to any member of the team who might have spoken out against him, for example in objecting to the timing of a patient's discharge from hospital. As a result of this there were few direct challenges of the consultant but frequent outbreaks of arguing within the team, although never during the ward round itself. Team morale had been low, especially among the most junior members. The arrival of the challenging social worker had meant that the rest of the team were spared the

direct anger of the consultant and also that of one another,
at least temporarily. This formed the basis of their tacit
acquiescence to the argument being enacted by just two team
members.

Observational learning, from witnessing such events as those
reported in the case studies, provides junior doctors with models
of more or less effective team functioning, especially from watching doctors who are in more senior and leadership positions.
An ability to understand the complex interaction of public and
personal levels of clinical team interaction is important. It helps
the student to assimilate appropriate lessons concerning successful leadership and team-membership skills, a mix of which is
required of doctors in almost all postgraduate medical settings.
As a potential future leader of the clinical team, the doctor needs
to recognize what it is like to be caught up in team difficulties
when agreed team goals are not being achieved and to be able to
identify and creatively deal with, or else avoid, 'cracks' and 'splits'
(see pp. 102–8). The junior doctor's schooling in the clinical
transaction model permits an understanding of the part played
by the wider hospital and non-hospital context, including the
psychosocial context of the patient.

Mrs Weber
In the team working with elderly patients, one particular
debate between the consultant and social worker concerned
Mrs Weber, a patient who suffered from a mild multi-infarct
dementia and from the effects of various other 'stroke'
phenomena. Her remaining son, with whom Mrs Weber lived,
himself had a learning disability. Together they had managed
to keep house for some years following the death of the father
from carcinoma of the larynx. During the mother's current
admission to hospital the son had also been hospitalized on
account of a myocardial infarction.

The social worker did not believe that the consultant
adequately appreciated the mutual dependency of mother and
son and how far the latter's absence from the house (or return
in a less than physically fit state) could jeopardize the
mother's social adjustment. She felt it her duty to represent
this view and, anticipating disagreement from the consultant,

made her case particularly vehemently. Unfortunately, this included a rather spiteful attack on what she perceived as her colleague's blinkered 'medical model' thinking. She implied that he was a particularly notable proponent of such narrow thinking. The consultant responded as anticipated and the familiar battle cycle had begun again.

Battles are particularly likely to occur where the team does not agree a clear objective for a given patient; where team culture is not attended to; where leadership may not be an agreed issue among team members; and where individual professional contributions differ but are not valued, especially by the leader. Successful teams may take for granted attention to such aspects of team functioning. The absence of such attention, however, often leaves much lingering resentment in terms of the perception of inequity of workload and an unfair distribution of cases.

In particular, the team may be divided into those perceived to be providing only a 'consultancy' (often the medical members) and those who see themselves as having to carry a continuing case responsibility (often non-medical members). In the example, it was this latter scenario which fuelled much of the disagreement between consultant and social worker. The latter felt that the consultant chose to define his medical responsibility very narrowly and she resented her own responsibilities which carried over from the hospital into the wider community following the discharge of a given patient.

By the end of the pre-registration year, the complex web of interacting systems and the myriad ways these can influence the clinical transaction will be appreciated, provided the complexity of the clinical transaction model and its ramifications are well understood.

Postgraduate training

How the clinical transaction model may continue to influence and inform training at the postgraduate level depends particularly upon the setting in which the doctor practices. In some settings, the clinical team is prominent (for example with children, elderly people, learning disabled or mentally ill patients) and, as a consequence, aspects relating to team function are to the fore. Because of the inevitable complexity of the team situation, and regardless of the setting, further training and discussion are beneficial. In some inpatient psychotherapeutic settings, however, there is a need to have staff team structures explicitly designed to evaluate this complexity (see Chapter 7). Training placements in such clinical settings can boost the relevant learning and also have wider application in those settings which do not routinely provide them.

Dr Marlowe

A psychiatric senior house officer in an inpatient psychotherapy unit was shocked by the amount of open disagreement witnessed among team members, not in front of patients, but in what she felt was the inappropriately named weekly 'staff sensitivity' meeting. At the start of Dr Marlowe's six months' placement it seemed to her that staff were being insensitive to one another. Gradually, however, she realized that the apparently wounding comments exchanged in the staff meeting did not impair professional or personal relationships. Indeed, in the clinical setting, these relationships were often straightforward because of the direct and open exchanges. She felt that the fact that the meeting was facilitated by a skilled group psychotherapist, who was outside of the hospital organization, was probably an important ingredient for its success. She contrasted the relatively high morale of this staff team with those of other teams in which she had been based, which were much less direct in their style of communication although superficially more kindly.

So far, most of the situations we have referred to are those found in hospital settings. However, many of the same principles of working in teams and learning from them, apply to GP practices, community-based mental health centres or day hospitals. In some of the latter they may not be so visible and yet they are still present and potentially influential. To an extent it is arbitrary where the boundaries of teams or systems are drawn but an analysis of the complex multipersonal situation, along the same lines, can yield useful insights into how the wider institution or department functions. This is likely to be most relevant when trying to decide how to manage a situation in which a team has become dysfunctional and is failing to achieve its public level goals.

Teaching process

Training regarding the clinical transaction model requires different processes of teaching at different stages of training. At the pre-clinical stage it may consist largely of didactic teaching of theory via the lecture and seminar format and does not require a change in existing techniques. Newer, problem-based curricula, however, involving learning in small groups may be even better suited to teaching this model. Videotaped clinical transactions relevant to the particular stage of training can be used in either situation to exemplify the main points of theory. At the pre-clinical stage, this essentially involves the recognition of the two types of clinical transaction – straightforward and complicated. However, it may also be helpful to introduce the notion of the transaction window, at this relatively early stage, in order to emphasize and demonstrate the interplay between public and personal levels of interaction between doctors and patients in the clinical transaction.

By the time of the clinical stage of training, methods concerned with the teaching of the clinical transaction model should include actual medical student–patient interaction. Traditional teaching methods, including the supervision from a trainer, augmented by observational learning from peers and seniors, are appropriate. The use of the transaction window in aiding the analysis of the clinical transaction, can be expanded to include 'systems' windows, which help analyse the effects of external overlapping or hierarchical systems. This enables clinical students to integrate information concerning the psychosocial aspects of their patients with the medical condition and its sequelae. The teaching of such aspects can be on an individual basis, between the individual student and trainer, or via small, problem-based learning groups. As indicated earlier, small group work has the advantage of enabling clinical students to become aware of their own public and personal level distinguishing features, especially in connection with their peers.

A suitably focused and facilitated group enables important discussion and elucidation of aspects of students' training experience. For example, the group might discuss difficulties arising from being taught and questioned in front of patients whom they have clerked, that is with whom they have engaged in a clinical transaction. In this situation students may feel a divided obligation to two transactions, the clinical transaction and the teaching transaction. Issues raised might include students' anxieties about discussing, in front of patients, clinical material necessary for the public level of the teaching transaction. They may display a reticence, out of a (personal level) consideration for the patient, which they fear, however, might jeopardize the good opinion of the trainers. There are likely to be many complex feelings arising in the relationship between students and their trainers. Appropriate discussion helps remove those feelings which obstruct the flow of learning. Role play techniques, use of audiotape and videotape, can also be utilized.

Postgraduate training represents a logical extension of clinical student training but requires a separate focus. The method of teaching depends upon the clinical setting in which the doctor is working. The form of teaching also depends on whether doctors are already familiar with the concepts associated with the clinical transaction model and upon the availability and cooperation of clinical colleagues who are similarly informed. When doctors are locked into a complicated clinical transaction with a patient it can be useful to discuss such a situation with colleagues. Reviewing the clinical transaction can be either as required or as part of a routine monitoring of complicated transactions. In the latter case regular meetings can be established solely to discuss them. Such a system has particular advantages in connection with prevention and early detection of such transactions (see Norton and Smith 1994). This is especially true of settings which are likely to generate complicated clinical transactions, such as those involving so-called 'complex' cases. Regular meetings, however, may not be feasible for all doctors who are interested in applying such concepts.

Assessment

In order to guarantee that training in the clinical transaction model is taking place, it is important for the relevant aspects to be monitored and also formally examined, as part of the relevant level of qualifying examinations. Like the assessment of clinical skills, intrinsic counselling skills can also be problematic to assess, regardless of the level of training. The theoretical aspects of the clinical transaction model and the related intrinsic counselling techniques, by contrast, can be tested by traditional methods, including multiple choice questions, short answer questions, essay or viva voce.

The practical application of intrinsic counselling skills is hard to assess or examine formally, partly because it represents specific attitudes and aspects of the doctor's individual professional style. In part, the difficulty stems from the fact that a complicated clinical transaction is the result of a unique combination and interplay of patient and clinician factors. Hence the candidate cannot be presented with a complicated clinical transaction unless this has been artificially arranged, for example, through an actor playing the part of a patient. The artificiality introduced thereby can clearly impair the validity of the assessment process. However, it is possible to envisage the use of surrogate patients, performing in such a way as to test the relevant skills.

The presentation of videotaped consultations is now a routine part of summative assessment at the end of vocational training for general practice (Campbell *et al.* 1995; Campbell and Murray 1996). Examiners versed in the clinical transaction model thereby have ample material to assess how candidates deal with potential minor departures from the straightforward clinical transaction. They also have a more formal method of identifying whether or not a consultation has failed in its objectives and become complicated.

An alternative method of assessment is to use appropriately selected or constructed videotaped interactions between doctors and patients (or surrogate patients) which can be shown to candidates, as brief clinical vignettes. Examination candidates can then discuss with examiners how to construe, in terms of the clinical transaction model, the observed clinician–patient interaction with a specific focus on the identification of public and personal domains and their hypothesized interplay. Candidates can also discuss where they might logically intervene if faced with such a complicated clinical transaction and demonstrate their knowledge and skills in using and applying the clinical transaction and systems windows. Thus, ways of managing complicated clinical transactions can be appropriately discussed and assessed.

Conclusions

Increasingly, it is recognized that doctors at the pre-qualifying stages require detailed training in communication and other non-clinical skills (GMC 1993). The inclusion of intrinsic counselling skills among the relevant clinical skills needed by doctors would necessarily require a change to existing training. In order to reach the whole field of medicine, training would need to be delivered at pre-clinical, clinical and postgraduate stages. Each stage would require a different approach and the content of these could be developed as training progresses.

Pre-clinical teaching about interpersonal consultation skills is at a theoretical level and introduces the student to relevant aspects of psychology and sociology. Introducing the clinical transaction model to students at this stage involves little or no change to the existing teaching structures and processes and only a minimal change in focus. Newer, problem-based curricula would seem to be readily adaptable to this purpose. At the clinical student stage, there is greater opportunity to exploit the natural groups, especially student peer groups, in which students find themselves. This serves to develop a sensitive understanding of the differences between public and personal level interactions. Also at this stage, the involvement of actual patients enables the relevant aspects to be discussed. Such peer group influences are similarly appropriate at the postgraduate level assuming that there is sufficient interest in and an acknowledgement of the relevance of such skills.

In order to secure a place for the clinical transaction model and associated intrinsic counselling skills in the medical curriculum formal assessment is necessary. The acquisition of intrinsic counselling skills can thus be examined via a mixture of traditional and new methods without creating undue amounts of extra work or bureaucracy to the examination system.

Chapter **9**

Closing comments

> These [GMC] documents emphasise what might be called the 'softer side of medicine', communication, ethical behaviour, treating patients with dignity, and being a team player. All medical students have met the stereotype of the brilliant diagnostician or the outstanding surgeon who is rude to patients, bullies students, and exploits colleagues. It may still be possible to be such a creature and be a successful conductor, footballer, or poet, but it's not acceptable in medicine. Patients and the public expect much more and doctors must deliver'.
>
> (Richard Smith 1998: 1623)

Introduction

Our intention here is to review some of the important features of the clinical transaction model which relate to intrinsic counselling skills and to the 'softer side of medicine' (R. Smith 1998). We also explore, from a psychoanalytic perspective, obstacles to doctors individually acquiring these skills and to the delivery of relevant training in medicine collectively.

Training priorities

The two-level model of the clinical transaction has far-reaching implications for professional training (see Chapter 8). Keeping in touch with what is happening at each of the interdependent levels, however, can be a demanding task. It requires doctors to consider and face, both in themselves and in their patients, the anxiety which is evoked by disease and any secondary physical, psychological or social handicap. Doctors also need to be aware of how aspects of their own personalities might gel or clash with those of their patients, how they react and respond to a particular diagnosis or illness and how these two elements might combine in a given clinical transaction. If necessary, doctors should be willing to modify their ways of relating to patients in order to preserve or restore a straightforward clinical transaction.

Facing anxiety, enhancing self–other awareness and modifying interpersonal behaviour are none of them easily achieved, although such tasks are easier for some doctors than for others. The tasks are nonetheless essential to clear and sensitive communication with patients and to the establishment of effective and dignified working relationships with them, their families and with professional colleagues. Attributes such as being able to communicate clearly are not unalterable givens but are skills which can be developed and enhanced through training. They can also be lost when doctors are working in circumstances which, for whatever reasons, they personally find too demanding. In the UK, these important skills have gained a high place on the list of essential educational objectives, at all levels of medical training (GMC 1993; R. Smith 1998). They do not, however, compete well in the crowded curriculum of medical education despite the fact that 'deficiencies in this area are responsible for a high proportion of complaints and misunderstandings' (GMC 1993).

Resistance and defensiveness

Recognition of the full importance of the ability to communicate well and to build effective relationships with patients entails the implicit acceptance of a two-level model of the clinical transaction and of the value of the intrinsic counselling skills with which to monitor it. That this is so has been acknowledged for many years, particularly since the work of Michael Balint (1964), and raises the question why training in these skills, at least within the main body of the medical curriculum, is still so inadequate – and a book such as this still relevant. Answers to these questions are necessarily speculative. It would seem that among many doctors, however, there is a resistance to giving such matters the time and attention they merit. It is therefore worth exploring some of the possible psychological origins of this resistance.

Resistance implies an opposing force. In psychoanalytic use, 'resistance' is a technical term which refers to 'the opposition encountered during psychoanalytic treatment to the process of making unconscious processes conscious' and in most cases 'is a manifestation of defence' (Rycroft 1968: 142–3). Such defences are unconsciously instigated to protect the self from excessive anxiety. According to psychoanalytic theory, anxiety can derive from three sources:

- an increase in instinctual tension (for example, the unconscious emergence of sexual feelings or behaviour within a clinical transaction)
- 'bad conscience' or threats to self-esteem (for example, arising out of misdiagnosis, treatment failure or rejection of the doctor's advice)
- realistic danger (for example, related to disease, including incapacity and the threat to the patient's life or, alternatively, the threat of actual violence from a dissatisfied patient).

Rather than face the anxiety from any of the above sources, defences are erected – some individual, some collective. The combined effect is a resistance to the acquisition of skills which, by their nature, inevitably involve an acceptance and exploration of anxiety and its sources. This is possibly the basis of the defensive situation within medicine which opposes and obstructs the learning and effective deployment of intrinsic counselling skills.

Individual defences

For the most part, defences against anxiety are helpful to the individual in that they facilitate day-to-day living and prevent a sense of being continually overwhelmed by anxiety. For example, some doctors, particularly surgeons, routinely carry out difficult and potentially hazardous procedures. To do so, they may avoid becoming personally overinvolved with their patients or their patients' personal experience of disease, since this may distract them from the highly technical aspects of their work. They are therefore helped to perform their professional task by the unconscious deployment of psychological defence mechanisms which have the effect of emotionally detaching them from their patients. The result may be that they appear aloof from or out of touch with patients (see the case of Mrs Brown, pp. 24–34).

In other situations defence mechanisms can operate counter-productively in the clinical transaction. In the case of Mrs Bradley (pp. 00–00), the doctor was unable for some time to confront the therapeutic stalemate that existed. It was as if she unconsciously defended herself against experiencing the anxiety caused by her feelings of irritation with Mrs Bradley, feelings which her conscience told her were inappropriate in a 'good' doctor.

Collective defences

Doctors work for the most part in teams or larger organizations. The public level tasks with which health care teams or organizations are engaged potentially raise profound anxieties common to those who work in them. Within medical institutions the major anxiety is provoked by disease and with it the fear of premature loss of life – death anxiety (Obholzer 1994). Collective mechanisms of defence develop to protect workers against these anxieties. Within the workplace, defences are likely to become organized in the form of shared attitudes and collectively pursued and rigidly defined procedures and routines with the unconscious goal of avoiding the conscious experience of anxiety, especially 'death anxiety' (Jaques 1955; Menzies 1970; de Board 1978).

A familiar example of such collective defence is the tendency of hospital staff to depersonalize people who are admitted as inpatients. It is as if the minimizing of the staff's personal involvement automatically optimizes professional detachment (which is deemed necessary) and is therefore justifiable. The operation of defence mechanisms can also preserve 'good feeling' in and between doctors or within the whole clinical team but at the expense of the denigration of the patient. In another common situation, the referred patient is maintained as 'good', i.e. deserving of help and treatment, but at the expense of the referrer or the patient's family, who are construed as 'bad' – as if by design or neglect they had created the patient's predicament.

Last words

Returning to the problem of the overcrowded curriculum, the fact that complaints about overloading go back well over a hundred years (GMC 1993) testifies to an extreme resistance to efforts to change it. With respect to finding adequate time to teach and learn about intrinsic counselling skills, it is possible to interpret the overcrowdedness itself as the result of a collective defence. Excessive attention to issues of medical fact and technical procedure is justifiable because these are felt to be 'vital' and must therefore be prioritized. The situation achieved, however, is one in which there is little time and mental energy left to confront those anxieties (especially concerning death) raised by the personal and interpersonal implications of disease. Experiencing those anxieties is thus avoided.

Through an understanding of the difficulties that anxiety and other interpersonal factors create, when patients and doctors meet, doctors are helped to maintain and restore the straightforwardness of the clinical transaction. To achieve this understanding and acquire the relevant intrinsic counselling skills, however, more space and time is needed in the medical curriculum for teaching about and training in these aspects of the clinical transaction. Because interpersonal elements exert an influence on each and every occasion when people interact, there are numerous educational opportunities for learning about them. A theoretical framework, such as provided by the clinical transaction model, helps to define educational objectives in relation to 'communication, ethical behaviour, treating patients with dignity, and being a team player' (R. Smith 1998). To the extent that understanding is deepened, it also helps to reduce the resistance to dealing with the difficult psychological matter which it addresses. Overcoming this resistance might well result in fewer complicated clinical transactions, more effective teamwork and so would benefit patients and doctors alike.

References

Argyle, M. (1988) *Bodily Communication*, 2nd edn. London: Methuen.

Armstrong, D. (1986) Illness behaviour revisited, in J.H. Lacey and D.A. Sturgeon (eds) *Proceedings of the 15th European Conference on Psychosomatic Research*. London: John Libbey.

Asher, R. (1972) *Richard Asher Talking Sense*. London: Pitman Medical.

Balint, M. (1964) *The Doctor, his Patient and the Illness*, 2nd edn. London: Pitman Medical.

Barclay, C. (1998) Intimate examinations without tears. *Trends in Urology, Gynaecology and Sexual Health* 3: 25–8.

Beattie, A. (1991) Knowledge and control in health promotion: a test case for social policy and social theory, in J. Gabe, M. Calnan and M. Bury (eds) *The Sociology of the Health Service*. London: Routledge.

Beauchamp, D. (1997) Lifestyle, public health and paternalism, in M. Sidell, L. Jones, J. Katz and A. Peberdy (eds) *Debates and Dilemmas in Promoting Health*. London: Macmillan with the Open University.

Bird, J., Hall, A., Maguire, P. and Heavy, A. (1993) Workshops for consultants in the teaching of clinical communication skills. *Medical Education* 27: 181–5.

Blaxter, M. (1990) *Health and Lifestyles*. London: Routledge.

Board, R. de (1978) *The Psychoanalysis of Organizations*. London: Routledge.

Brody, H. (1987) *Stories of Sickness*. New Haven and London: Yale University Press.

Buckman, R. (1992) How to Break Bad News: a Guide for Health-case Professionals. London: Papermac.

Burnard, P. (1989) *Counselling Skills for Health Professionals*. London: Chapman & Hall.

Byrne, P. and Long, B.E.L. (1976) *Doctors Talking to Patients*. London: HMSO.

Campbell, L.M. and Murray, T.S. (1996) Summative assessment of vocational trainees: results of a three year study. *British Journal of General Practice* **46**: 411–14.

Campbell, L.M., Howie, J.G.R. and Murray, T.S. (1995) Use of videotaped consultations in summative assessment of trainees in general practice. *British Journal of General Practice* **45**: 137–41.

Cole, E. (1990) Introduction, in *Lifestyle, Health and Health Promotion*. Proceedings of a symposium on health and lifestyle. Cambridge: Health Promotion Research Trust.

Corney, R. (1993) A need for counselling skills in general practice. *Journal of the Royal Society of Medicine* **86**: 425–7.

Curtis-Jenkins, G. (1996) *A Guide to Counselling in General Practice*. Counselling in Primary Care Trust.

Curzon, L.B. (1990) *Teaching in Further Education: An Outline of Principles and Practice*. London: Cassell.

Department of Health (1991) *The Patient's Charter*. London: HMSO.

Department of Health (1992) *The Health of the Nation*, Cm 1986. London: HMSO.

DHSS (1977) *Prevention and Health*, Cmnd 7047. London: HMSO.

DHSS (1987) *Promoting Better Health*, Cm 249. London: HMSO.

Fabb, W.E. and Marshall, J.R. (1983) *The Assessment of Clinical Competence in General Family Practice*. Lancaster: MTP Press.

Farrall, W. (1993) Differing approaches to training and practice in counselling. *Journal of the Royal Society of Medicine* **86**: 424–5.

Fraser, R.C. (ed.) (1987) *Clinical Method: A General Practice Approach*. London: Butterworths.

Gabbard, G.O. (1986) The treatment of the 'special' patient in a psychoanalytic hospital. *International Review of Psychoanalysis* **13**: 333–47.

General Medical Council (GMC) (1993) *Tomorrow's Doctors*. London: GMC.

Groves, J.E. (1978) Taking care of the hateful patient. *New England Journal of Medicine* **298**: 883–5.

Heaton, C.J. and Marquez, J.T. (1990) Patient preferences for physician gender in the male genital/rectal exam. *Family Practice Research Journal* **10**: 105–15.

Heron, J. (1975) *Six Categories of Intervention Analysis*. Guildford: University of Surrey.

Horder, J. and Moore, G.T. (1990) The consultation and outcome. *British Journal of General Practice* **40**: 442–3.

Horton, J.A., Clance, P.R., Sterk-Elifson, C. and Emshoff, J. (1995) Touch in psychotherapy: a survey of patients' experiences. *Psychotherapy* **32**: 443–57.

Innui, T., Yourte, E.L. and Williamson, J.W. (1976) Improved outcome in hypertension after physician tutorials. *Annals of Internal Medicine* **84**: 646–51.

Jacobs, M. (1988) *Psychodynamic Counselling in Action*. London: SAGE.

Jaques, E. (1955) Social systems as a defence against persecutory and depressive anxiety, in M. Klein, P. Heimann and R. Money-Kyrle (eds) *New Directions in Psychoanalysis*. London: Tavistock.

Ko Ko, J. (1993) Education for medical practice of tomorrow. Proceedings of the World Summit of Medical Education, Edinburgh. *Medical Education* **28** (supplement 1): 54–61.

Kravitz, R.L., Callahan, E.J., Paterniti, D., Antonius, D., Dunham, M. and Lewis, C.E. (1996) Prevalence and sources of patients' unmet expectations for care. *Annals of Internal Medicine* **125**: 730–7.

Larsen, M., Oldeide, C.C. and Malterud, K. (1997) Women's experiences of pelvic examinations. *Family Practitioner* **14**: 148–52.

McAvoy, B.R. and McAvoy, P.A. (1981) in J. Cormack, M. Marinker and D. Morrell (eds) *Teaching General Practice*. London: Kluwer Medical.

McEvoy, P. (1993) *Educating the Future GP*. Oxford: Radcliffe Medical Press.

McLeod, J. (1993) *An Introduction to Counselling*. Buckingham: Open University Press.

MacNaughton, J. (1995) Anecdotes and empiricism. *British Journal of General Practice* **45**: 571–2.

McWhinney, I.R. (1981) *An Introduction to Family Medicine*. Oxford: Oxford University Press.

Main, T. (1957) The ailment. *British Journal of Medical Psychology* **30**: 129–45.

Mechanic, D. (1962) The concept of illness behaviour. *Journal of Chronic Diseases* **15**: 189–94.

Menzies, I.E.P. (1970) *The Functioning of Social Systems as a Defence against Anxiety*. Centre for Applied Social Research. London: Tavistock Institute of Human Relations.

Metcalfe, D. (1989) Teaching communication skills to medical students, in D. Seedhouse and A. Cribb (eds) *Changing Ideas in Health Care*. Chichester: John Wiley.

Miller, L.J. (1989) In-patient management of borderline personality disorder: review and update. *Journal of Personality Disorders* **3**: 122–34.

Morley, C. (1997) The use of denial by patients with cancer. *Professional Nurse* **12**: 380–1.

Morris, C. (1964) *Signification and Significance*. Cambridge, Mass.: MIT Press.

Myerscough, P.R. (1992) *Talking with Patients: A Basic Clinical Skill*. Oxford: Oxford University Press.

Nettleton, S. (1995) *The Sociology of Health and Illness*. Cambridge: Polity Press.

Norton, K. (1996) Management of difficult personality disorder patients. *Advances in Psychiatric Treatment* **2**: 202–10.

Norton, K. and McGauley, G. (1998) *Counselling Difficult Clients*. London: SAGE.

Norton, K. and Smith, S. (1994) *Problems with Patients: Managing Complicated Transactions*. Cambridge: Cambridge University Press.

Obholzer, A. (1994) Managing social anxieties in public sector organisations, in A. Obholzer and V.Z. Roberts (eds) *The Unconscious at Work: Individual and Organisational Stresses in the Human Services*. London: Routledge.

O'Dowd, T.C. (1988) Five years of heartsink patients in general practice. *British Medical Journal* **287**: 528–30.

Pendleton, D.A. and Hasler, J. (eds) (1983) *Doctor–Patient Communication*. London: Academic Press.

Pendleton, D.A., Schofield, T., Tate, P. and Havelock, P. (1984) *The Consultation: An Approach to Learning and Teaching*. Oxford: Oxford University Press.

Phongsavan, P., Ward, J.E., Oldenburg, B.F. and Gordon, J.J. (1995) Mental health practices and educational needs of general practitioners. *Medical Journal of Australia* **162**: 139–42.

Plato (1987) *Early Socratic Dialogues*. Harmondsworth: Penguin.

Preston-Whyte, E. (1987) Doctor–patient communication, in R.C. Fraser (ed.) *Clinical Method: A General Practice Approach*. London: Butterworths.

RCOG (1997) *Report of a Working Party*. London: RCOG Press.

Roberts, H. (1985) *Women: The Patient Patients*. London: Pandora Press.

Rycroft, C. (1968) *A Critical Dictionary of Psychoanalysis*. Harmondsworth: Penguin.

Schrire, S. (1986) Frequent attenders – a review. *Family Practitioner* **3**: 272–5.

Sidell, M., Jones, L., Katz, J. and Peberdy, A. (1997) *Debates and Dilemmas in Promoting Health*. London: Macmillan with the Open University.

Smith, R. (1998) Renegotiating medicine's contract with patients: the GMC is leading the way. *British Medical Journal* **316**: 1622–3.

Smith, S. (1997) The 'difficult' patient, in C.R.K. Hind (ed.) *Communication Skills in Medicine*. London: British Medical Journal.

Smith, S. (1998) Postmodernity and a hypertensive patient: rescuing value from nihilism. *Journal of Medical Ethics* **24**: 25–31.

Sontag, S. (1977) *Illness as Metaphor*. Harmondsworth: Penguin.

Stott, N.C.H. and Davis, R.H. (1979) The exceptional potential in each primary care consultation. *Journal of the Royal College of General Practitioners* **29**: 201–5.

Tones, K. (1997) Health education as empowerment, in M. Sidell, L. Jones, J. Katz and A. Peberdy (eds) *Debates and Dilemmas in Promoting Health*. London: Macmillan with the Open University.

Townsend, P. and Davidson, N. (1982) *Inequalities in Health: The Black Report*. Harmondsworth: Penguin.

Tuckett, D.A., Boulton, M., Olson, C. and Williams, A. (1986) *Meetings between Experts: An Approach to Sharing Ideas in Medical Consultations*. London: Tavistock.

Weaver, J.J. (1997) Intimate exposure during childbirth: do women care and do they cope? Paper presented at BPS annual conference, Edinburgh, 4 April.

WHO (1986) *Ottawa Charter for Health Promotion*. Health and Welfare, Canada.

Wilkinson, C. (1989) Uninterrupted speaking of patient in general practice and consultant clinic. *British Medical Journal* 319: 1728–30.

Wright, H.J. and MacAdam, D.B. (1979) *Clinical Thinking and Practice: Diagnosis and Decision in Patient Care*. Edinburgh: Churchill Livingstone.

Index